NoLex 1·13

EVERYTHING YOU NEED TO KNOW ABOUT WORLD HISTORY HOMEWORK

A Desk Reference for Students and Parents

Anne Zeman and Kate Kelly

FOURTH TO SIXTH GRADES

Design: Bennett Gewirtz, Gewirtz Graphics, Inc.
Illustration: Moffitt Cecil

For their assistance in the preparation of this manuscript, grateful acknowledgment to Betty Holmes, Director of UFT's Dial-A-Teacher, Vincent Ridge, and Carmen Edgerly. Dial-A-Teacher is a collaborative program of the United Federation of Teachers and the New York City Board of Education. Many thanks also to Steven Deyle of the University of California at Davis Department of History for fact-checking.

Grateful acknowledgment is made to:
    FPG International, for permission to reprint photographs on pages 37, 67, and 94.
    The Library of Congress, for permission to reprint photographs on pages 95, 98, 100, and 101.
    The Scholastic Picture Research Department, for permission to reprint photographs on pages 31, 35, 47, 52, 54, 67, 70, 90, 94, 99, and 101 (photo, Hideki Tojo).

Library of Congress Cataloging-in-Publication Data

Zeman, Anne, 1951-
    Everything you need to know about world history homework / Anne
        Zeman and Kate Kelly.
        p. cm. — (Scholastic homework reference series)
    Includes index.
    ISBN 0-590-49364-7
    1. World History—Juvenile literature.
    I. Kelly, Kate. II. Title. III. Series.
    021.Z44 1994
    909—dc20   94-25438
                                            CIP
                                            AC

12 11 10 9 8 7 6 5 4 3 2 1   4 5 6 7 8 9/9

Printed in the U.S.A.   09
First Scholastic printing, August 1995

CONTENTS

INTRODUCTION

It's homework time — but you have questions. Just how did your teacher ask you to do the assignment? You need help, but your parents are busy, and you can't reach your classmate on the phone. Where can you go for help?

What Questions Does This Book Answer?

In *Everything You Need to Know About World History Homework,* you will find a wealth of information, including the answers to ten of the most commonly asked world history and world cultures homework questions.

1. Where is the Fertile Crescent, and what happened there? The Fertile Crescent and the civilization it supported are described on pages 2–5.

2. When were the great pyramids of Egypt built, and what was their purpose? Find out about the great pyramids on pages 11 and 12.

3. What was Hammurabi's Code, and on what principles was it based? Hammurabi's Code is explained on page 4.

4. Where and when were the first Olympic Games? The Olympic Games is the subject of a feature on page 17.

5. What is a democracy? A direct democracy? An indirect democracy? The principle of democracy is clarified on pages 16 and 18.

6. Where were the first civilizations in India? A history of early India is found on pages 26-30.

7. Which of the world's three major religions developed in the Middle East? The major world religions that sprang from the Middle East are described on pages 38–42.

8. What was the gold-salt trade? Where did it take place? The gold-salt trade is described on page 44.

9. What was feudalism like in Europe and in Japan? Feudalism is explained on pages 36, 73, and 86.

10. What is capitalism? What is communism? Capitalism and communism are compared on page 90.

What Is the Scholastic Homework Reference Series?

The Scholastic Homework Reference Series is a set of unique reference resources written especially to answer the homework questions of fourth, fifth, and sixth graders. The series provides ready information to answer commonly asked homework questions in a variety of subjects. Here you'll find facts, charts, definitions, and explanations, complete with examples and illustrations that will supplement schoolwork colorfully, clearly—and comprehensively.

A Note to Parents

The information for the Scholastic Homework Reference Series was gathered from current textbooks, national curricula, and the invaluable assistance of the UFT Dial-A-Teacher staff. Dial-A-Teacher, a collaborative program of the United Federation of Teachers and the New York City Board of Education, is a telephone service available to elementary school students in New York City. Telephone lines are open during the school term from 4:00 to 7:00 P.M., Monday to Thursday, by dialing 212-777-3380. Because of Dial-A-Teacher's success in New York City, similar organizations have been established in other communities across the country. Check to see if there's a telephone homework service in your area.

It's important to support your children's efforts to do homework. Welcome their questons and see that they are equipped with a well-lighted desk or table, pencils, paper, and any other books or equipment—such as rulers, calculators, reference or text books, and so on—that they may need. You might also set aside a special time each day for doing homework, a time when you're available to answer questions that may arise. But don't do your children's homework for them. Remember, homework should create a bond between school and home. It is meant to enhance on a daily basis the lessons taught at school, and to promote good work and study habits. Although it is gratifying to have your children present flawless homework papers, the flawlessness should be a result of your children's explorations and efforts—not your own.

The Scholastic Homework Reference Series is designed to help your children complete their homework on their own to the best of their abilities. If they're stuck, you can use these books with them to find answers to troubling homework problems. And, remember, when the work is done—praise your children for a job well done.

EVERYTHING YOU NEED TO KNOW ABOUT

WORLD HISTORY

HOMEWORK

ANCIENT HISTORY
(4000 B.C. – A.D. 500)

1 The Fertile Crescent

Civilization began in the area known as the Fertile Crescent. (A civilization is a human organization that involves a central government, permanent buildings, food production, and, sometimes, a system of writing.) The Fertile Crescent was a piece of land that stretched from the eastern shore of the Mediterranean Sea to the Persian Gulf. It got its name because the soil was rich, and it was shaped like a half-moon, or crescent.

The eastern section of the Fertile Crescent, between the Tigris and Euphrates rivers, was called *Mesopotamia*. Mesopotamia means "land between the rivers." The western part of the Fertile Crescent was called the *Mediterranean* section.

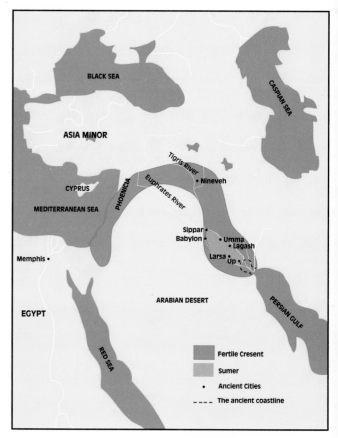

BLACK SEA

CASPIAN SEA

ASIA MINOR

Tigris River

Euphrates River

• Nineveh

CYPRUS

PHOENICIA

MEDITERRANEAN SEA

Sippar •
Babylon • • Umma
• Lagash
Larsa •
Ur •

Memphis •

ARABIAN DESERT

PERSIAN GULF

EGYPT

RED SEA

	Fertile Cresent
	Sumer
•	Ancient Cities
- - - -	The ancient coastline

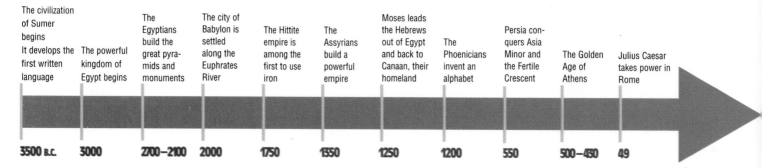

The civilization of Sumer begins It develops the first written language	The powerful kingdom of Egypt begins	The Egyptians build the great pyramids and monuments	The city of Babylon is settled along the Euphrates River	The Hittite empire is among the first to use iron	The Assyrians build a powerful empire	Moses leads the Hebrews out of Egypt and back to Canaan, their homeland	The Phoenicians invent an alphabet	Persia conquers Asia Minor and the Fertile Crescent	The Golden Age of Athens	Julius Caesar takes power in Rome
3500 B.C.	3000	2700–2100	2000	1750	1350	1250	1200	550	500–430	49

The Sumerians

In the southern part of Mesopotamia was an area known as Sumer. The Sumerians were one of the first people known to live in the Fertile Crescent. They lived there from about 3500 to 2000 B.C.

The Sumerians farmed and raised cattle. Many were tradespeople and artisans (craftspeople) who lived in cities. In the cities, the Sumerians built huge temples and monuments. They invented the arch and the *ziggurat*, a temple shaped like a pyramid with terraces and steps. One of their cities was called Ur. This city was found buried in sand in 1927, along with many graves and artifacts. The graves that were found turned out to be the tombs of kings. The people who unearthed these tombs, called *archaeologists*, discovered a number of things about the Sumerians:

- **They were skilled builders and artists.**

- **They had an alphabet and knew how to write.**

- **Their army was supplied with weapons.**

- **Their metals, stones, and wood were obtained from trading with other people.**

- **Kings were treated as gods who had great power and wealth.**

Sumer consisted of three classes of people. The upper class included kings, nobles, priests, wealthy landowners, and government officials. The middle class was made up of merchants, farmers, tradespeople, and soldiers. The lowest class was made up of slaves.

Accomplishments of the Sumerians

1 They developed the first written language, a system of writing called cuneiform. The alphabet consisted of about 500 characters, or wedge-shaped forms.

2 They studied science and mathematics. Their skills in mathematics were so developed that they created a system for subdividing a day and a year as well as dividing a circle into 360 parts.

3 They were skillful in using the wheel and made vehicles for farming, moving goods for trade, and fighting enemies.

The Babylonians

The city of Babylon was located on the Euphrates River. It was founded about 2000 B.C. and is part of present-day Iraq. Babylon became the capital of the empire of Babylonia and was an important center for trade and religious worship. The city included splendid temples to the *deities* (the gods and goddesses they worshiped).

One of the greatest kings of Babylon was *Hammurabi*, who ruled for 42 years, from 1792 to 1750 B.C. He was the first ruler to record a set of laws for his people. Hammurabi's Code of Laws consisted of 282 laws and was displayed in every town. Hammurabi based his laws on the principle that the strong should not injure the weak. These laws created a reasonable tax system, set fair prices and wages, acknowledged the rights of women (even allowing them to own property), and set up a strong system of punishments for the guilty.

Another famous king was *Nebuchadrezzar II*. He ruled Babylonia for 43 years, from 605 to 562 B.C., and is mentioned in the Bible, in the Book of Daniel. Nebuchadrezzar II conquered Jerusalem and forced thousands of people to move to Babylon to live in captivity. He also captured the cities of Tyre and Judah.

Nebuchadrezzar II spent enormous amounts of money in building up Babylon, and its Hanging Gardens eventually became a wonder of the ancient world (see p. 25). He is said to have gone mad toward the end of his life; Babylon grew weaker when he died.

Accomplishments of the Babylonians

1 They established a code of laws.

2 They believed in astrology, which holds that the movements of the stars and planets have a direct effect on human life. Their recognition of the different planets and stars led to the scientific study of astronomy, the study of the universe.

The Assyrians

Starting about 1350 B.C., the Assyrians lived in the area where the Sumerians had once lived. They were traders and fierce warriors who built a mighty empire by conquering others with their highly skilled army. When enemies were captured they were either taken as slaves or murdered. Sometimes the Assyrians destroyed entire cities, such as the conquered city of Elam in 640 B.C.

The Assyrians conquered the Fertile Crescent, including Babylon and Egypt. Their capital was at Nineveh. The empire grew wealthy from the cities the Assyrians captured and the taxes they collected from the defeated peoples.

The last great king of Assyria was *Ashurbanipal*. His library held a great deal of information about Assyria. It was the first known library and contained more than 22,000 clay tablets written in Sumerian cuneiform. These tablet "books" included proverbs, fables, folktales, as well as writings on religion, science, law, and magic.

The Assyrian Empire lasted over 700 years, to 612 B.C., when the Babylonians and the Medes destroyed Nineveh.

Accomplishments of the Assyrians

1 They built a system of roads.

2 They instituted a form of government for the provinces in which a governor was appointed to oversee the king's territory.

3 They established the first library.

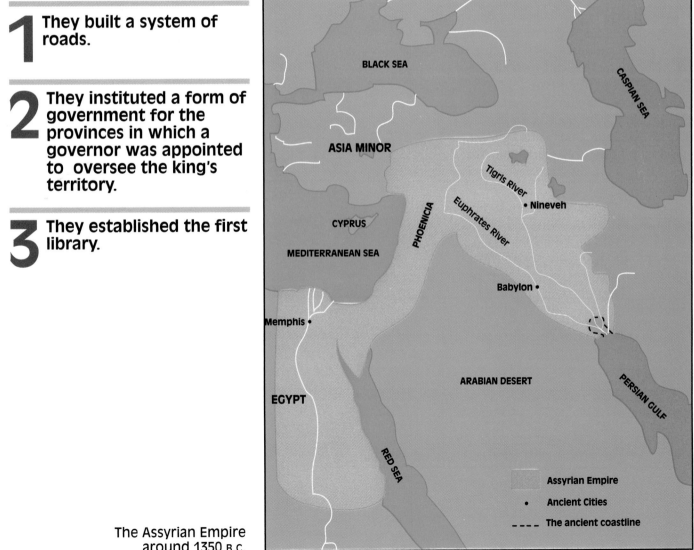

The Assyrian Empire around 1350 B.C.

The Hebrews

The Hebrews lived in Canaan, a narrow strip of land between the Mediterranean Sea and the Jordan River. Originally, they were nomads who wandered the land. When severe drought forced them into Egypt, the Egyptians made them slaves. Around 1250 B.C., their leader, *Moses*, led them out of Egypt and back to their homeland. This journey back is known as the *Exodus*, which means "going out."

After arriving in Canaan, the Hebrews lived in tribes, or groups. There were 12 tribes that lived separately until they banded together to fight an enemy invader. The leader who brought the tribes together was *Saul*. He defeated the Philistines and was named the first king. During the battle with the Philistines, a man named *David* killed *Goliath*, the powerful Philistine leader. This made David a hero, and he became king around 1000 B.C., after the death of Saul. David built Israel into the greatest power in the area. He named Jerusalem the capital. Jerusalem is also known as the City of David, and it has become one of the most influential cities of all time.

David's son *Solomon* became king about 961 B.C. He made Jerusalem an even greater city, building many monuments and palaces, including the magnificent *Temple of Jerusalem*. Both David and Solomon put heavy taxes on their people to pay for these buildings and to keep a large army. People began to resent the taxes. After Solomon's death, the citizens began to separate into tribes again, and eventually the north and south split. The northern Hebrews called their land the kingdom of *Israel*. The southern Hebrews called theirs the kingdom of *Judah*.

The Hebrews' religion is known as *Judaism*. They were unusual in that they worshiped only one God. This belief in one God later influenced Christianity as well as Islam, the religion of the Muslims.

The story of the ancient Hebrews (also called Israelites), along with their beliefs and prayers, is told in the Bible. According to the Bible, God gave Moses the Ten Commandments, the foundation of Judaism. These new religious rules set standards for goodness and moral behavior.

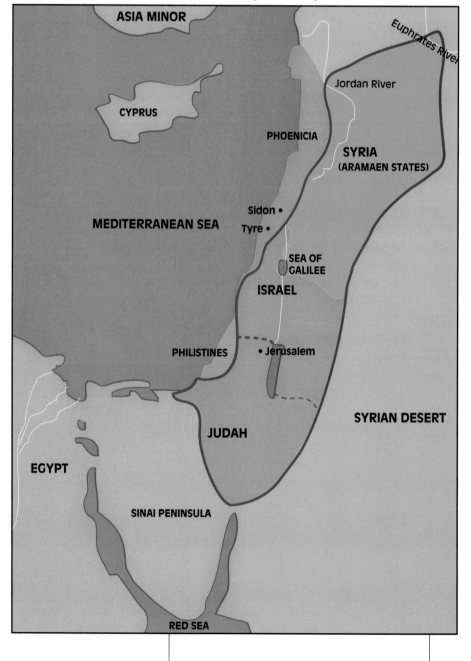

The Hebrews and Phoenicians shared a narrow strip of land along the eastern coast of the Mediterranean Sea.

Accomplishments of the Hebrews

1 They believed in a single all-powerful God.

2 They recorded the Bible.

3 Their high moral behavior, founded on the Ten Commandments, set new standards.

4 Their prophets fought for justice for the poor and weak.

The Phoenicians

The Phoenicians lived in small city-states along the Mediterranean coast, in present-day Lebanon, from about 1200 to 800 B.C. Tyre and Sidon were their chief cities. The Phoenicians were the most famous traders of the ancient world. They turned to trade because they had little land to farm. They were skilled shipbuilders and master sailors, becoming one of the first people to sail at night by the stars. The Phoenicians were also explorers. They sailed across the Mediterranean and built colonies such as Carthage in North Africa.

Many Phoenicians became wealthy. They controlled trade throughout the Mediterranean area for nearly 300 years. They traded their wool, papyrus, ivory, and glass for goods they needed. One of the products the Phoenicians were most known for was a vivid purple dye made from tiny shells. It was so expensive to make that only very wealthy people could buy purple cloth. It became the favorite color of royalty.

Accomplishments of the Phoenicians

1 They invented an alphabet. In order to keep business records of their trade, the Phoenicians developed a system of writing. The Phoenician alphabet contained 22 letters and, unlike cuneiform and hieroglyphics, the letters represented the sounds of the human voice. This made it much easier to read and write. Because the Phoenicians traveled so much, they spread the use of the alphabet to many places.

2 They developed artistic skills, such as carving ivory figures and making colored glass ornaments.

3 They traded all over the Mediterranean, spreading both their own goods and those of their trading partners.

The Persians

The Persians lived east of the Fertile Crescent on the plateau of Iran. They were warriors on horseback who came from central Asia. Their capital city was Persepolis. It was built by the *Achaemenid* family, who ruled the Persian Empire from 550 to 330 B.C. As rulers, the Persians were generous to the people they conquered.

Cyrus the Great ruled from 559 to 530 B.C. and expanded the Persian Empire by conquering Asia Minor and eventually the Fertile Crescent. Under King *Darius I*, the empire was extended eastward as far as the Indus River in India. It was during his reign that the building of Persepolis began. He was often called *Darius the Great* because he restored order and made many improvements to the empire. Because the empire was so large, Darius divided it into 20 provinces, each ruled by an official called a *satrap*. The government built roads to improve trade and the movement of the army. It also built a canal that connected the Nile River to the Red Sea.

Persia fought several wars with the Greek city-states (see p. 15). In 330 B.C., Persia fell to the army of *Alexander the Great* (see p. 19).

Accomplishments of the Persians

1 They divided their empire into provinces for easier rule.

2 They built roads and canals.

3 They wrote the Avesta, a religious book based on the beliefs of the prophet Zoroaster.

Zoroastrian priests carried a staff with a bull's head as a symbol of their religious battle against evil.

The Hittites

The Hittites lived in the mountains near modern Turkey. Their empire was established by 1750 B.C. and was known as **Hatti**. Its capital was **Hattusa**. Hattusa was 3,000 feet above sea level and surrounded by mountains as well as a stone wall up to 26 feet thick. The Hittites built a powerful empire that lasted about 550 years.

The Hittite rulers were the first to use a treaty to settle differences with other peoples. **King Hattusili III** and **King Ramses II** of Egypt signed a treaty in 1284 B.C. They agreed not to make war on each other, to help each other if attacked by a third party, and to respect each other's borders. It was one of the first treaties signed by two great empires.

Accomplishments of the Hittites

1 They were among the first people to use iron, which is easier to make than bronze. Before this, people used copper and bronze to make tools and weapons. This was one of the most important accomplishments of the ancient world.

2 They signed some of the first treaties.

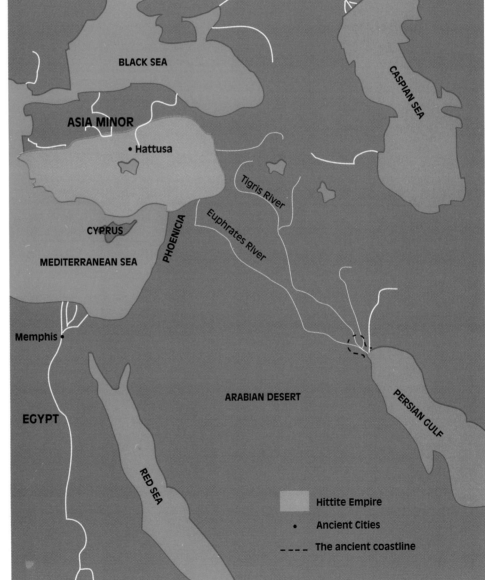

The Hittite Empire covered much of Asia Minor in present-day Turkey.

BLACK SEA

CASPIAN SEA

ASIA MINOR

• Hattusa

Tigris River

CYPRUS

Euphrates River

PHOENICIA

MEDITERRANEAN SEA

Memphis •

ARABIAN DESERT

PERSIAN GULF

EGYPT

RED SEA

◼ Hittite Empire
• Ancient Cities
---- The ancient coastline

2 The First Civilization of Ancient Egypt

Ancient Egypt was one of the earliest civilizations. It was located in northeast Africa and began about 5,000 years ago along the Nile River. Ancient Egyptian civilization lasted for about 3,000 years, from 3100 to 332 B.C.

Ancient Egypt was called "the gift of the Nile" (see p. 11). Egyptians depended on the river for food and work. The people worked together to build irrigation systems to bring water from the Nile to other fields for their crops.

The Egyptians were the first people to make paper, and theirs was the first civilization with a written history. Paper was made from papyrus reed. Ropes, mats, and even boats were also made from papyrus reed. Egyptians were also excellent engineers and builders. They built the great pyramids, temples, statues, and many other buildings. They forced thousands of slaves to work on these buildings.

The Egyptian language was based on *hieroglyphics*. The Egyptians wrote laws, books, prayers, and hymns. They also did mathematics and invented a calendar.

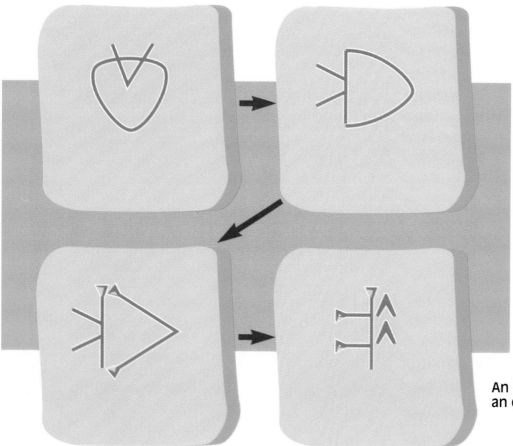

An early cuneiform symbol for an ox evolved from pictographs.

The Nile River

The Nile River was the center of life for the Egyptians. It is the longest river in the world. It starts in central Africa and flows 4,000 miles north to the Mediterranean Sea. Ancient Egyptian civilization began in the *Nile Delta*, where the river enters the Mediterranean Sea and forms a marshy plain of river mud.

Every year the Nile River flooded and left a rich layer of soil that was good for growing crops. This rich soil was very important to the Egyptians since there is a desert on both sides of the Nile, with little rainfall.

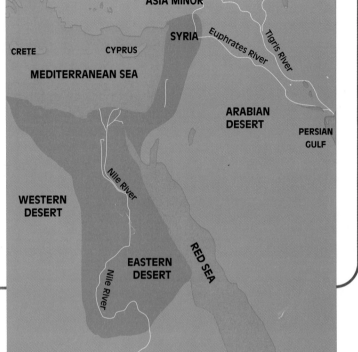

The Nile Delta

DAILY LIFE OF EGYPTIANS

Farming was the chief work in Egypt, and people learned to work the ground to produce wheat, barley, and vegetables. They used donkeys for heavy labor. The men also hunted wild animals and fished. Families lived in houses made of mud, brick, and wood. They often kept small farm animals, like goats or geese. Some raised cattle and sheep for food. Women wove linen and wool for clothing and cooked the meals. Bread and beer were main items in every home. Children helped in the farming and with the household chores.

Some people made crafts such as jewelry, tapestries, pottery, dishes, and metal objects. Others were scribes, the only people who knew how to write. They wrote with pens made from reeds on paper made from papyrus. Scribes usually worked for officials.

The king was regarded as a god and was very powerful. In Egypt the king was called the *pharaoh*. He (and, at least once, she) was considered the earthly leader of the gods. Egyptians worshiped many gods and built temples of brick and stone for them. The great pyramids were built as tombs for the pharaohs. When they died, the pharaohs and their treasures were put in the pyramids.

Builder's escape shaft

Passage way

Entrance

Underground room

The Kingdoms of Egypt

Before 3000 B.C., Egypt was divided into the kingdoms of Upper Egypt, in the Nile Delta, and Lower Egypt. *Menes*, a king from the south, conquered and joined the two lands. Menes was the first pharaoh. His was called the First Dynasty. A *dynasty* is a series of rulers from the same family.

Thirty dynasties ruled Egypt for 3,000 years. Most of the pharaohs were men. Usually, the only women who had important titles were priestesses. However, there was a female pharaoh—*Queen Hatshepsut*. She was the daughter of King *Thutmose I*. He was determined that she follow him, and he instructed the nobles of the royal court that she would be the next ruler. Hatshepsut became queen upon the death of her father, about 1500 B.C. She later took a husband, *Thutmose II*. After his death, she crowned herself King Hatshepsut and became pharaoh. During her reign, Egypt rose to great power and wealth. It was a golden age of peace and prosperity.

Because Egypt's history is so long, historians divide it into three periods—the Old Kingdom, the Middle Kingdom, and the New Kingdom.

Period	Date	Highlights
Old Kingdom	2700–2100 B.C.	The capital was Memphis. The great pyramids and the Sphinx, a large statue with a head of a man and body of a lion, were built.
Middle Kingdom	2100–1600 B.C.	Egyptian civilization reached great heights. Engineering projects like irrigation ditches and canals were built. Egypt was conquered by invaders but then recovered.
New Kingdom	1600–1100 B.C.	This era is also called the Empire, and the capital was Thebes. Egypt conquered many areas during this time. About 1100 B.C., its great power had begun to decline.

Akhenaten: The Pharaoh Who Worshiped One God

The pharaoh **Amenhotep IV** wanted the Egyptians to stop worshiping many **deities** (gods and goddesses). He wanted them to worship only one god, the sun god, **Aten**. He closed the great temple of Amon, "the king of gods," at Thebes. Amenhotep wanted to remove all aspects of Amon. To prove he was serious, Amenhotep changed his name to **Akhenaten**, which means "spirit of Aten." He even created a new capital city devoted to Aten. He named the city Akhetaton; it is known today as Tell al'Amarna.

Akhenaten, whose reign was roughly from 1370 to 1362 B.C., was one of the first people ever to believe in only one god. His people followed him, but the pharaohs, after his death, restored the old deities.

The Tomb of King Tutankhamen

In 1922 a great discovery was made — the tomb of the pharaoh **Tutankhamen**. Unlike other ancient tombs, this one had not been robbed because it was so well hidden. The magnificent treasures in the tomb gave new insight into ancient Egypt and the skilled work of its artists.

The tomb contained four rooms and each contained the king's personal possessions. There were thrones, beds, chariots, clothes, and statues of gods. Many of the items were made of gold, ivory, and precious stones. The coffin was the most magnificent. It was made of solid gold and contained a headpiece in the likeness of King Tutankhamen made of gold, ebony, and turquoise. This headpiece is considered one of the most beautiful treasures of the world and is on display in Cairo, Egypt.

Successor to Akhenaten, Tutankhamen became king when he was only nine years old. He ruled Egypt for only ten years. During his reign, he restored many temples and recognized the old gods. Very little is known of Tutankhamen's life. He died unexpectedly at 18 or 19 years of age, around 1350 B.C.

Accomplishments of the Egyptians

1 They made paper from the papyrus reed plant.

2 They invented a calendar.

3 They built the great pyramids.

4 They invented the shadoof, a cranelike device for lifting water from the Nile.

5 They used a loom to weave cloth for clothing.

6 They invented hieroglyphics, a system of writing using characters in the form of pictures.

Cleopatra

Cleopatra was queen of Egypt from 51 to 30 B.C. She was intelligent, charming, and ambitious. While the Roman military leader *Julius Caesar* (see p. 21) was in Egypt, he fell in love with her, and they had a child. She moved to Rome and they lived there until Caesar was killed. Cleopatra then returned to Egypt, where she married her brother, who was the ruler of Egypt. Cleopatra had her brother poisoned and became queen. Egypt had lost most of the power and riches it had during the rule of the pharaohs, and Cleopatra wanted to get them back.

Cleopatra met *Mark Antony*, another great Roman general. Mark Antony wanted to become the ruler of Rome, and Cleopatra saw this as an opportunity to expand her power. She wanted to rule the eastern half of the Roman Empire. As a result, important Romans refused to help Mark Antony, and *Octavian* (Augustus) became emperor. Mark Antony killed himself and later Cleopatra killed herself as well.

3 Ancient Greece

Greeks lived in southeast Europe over 2,000 years ago. They built Sparta, Athens, and other famous cities. Greece was divided into *city-states*. This meant that each city was like a separate, small nation, with its own laws and government. Even though the city-states operated independently, all of Greece shared the same language and culture. Although Greece had many city-states, the most famous and powerful were Athens and Sparta. They were located on the Peloponnesian Peninsula.

Early Greek States of Athens and Sparta

Athens and Sparta were strong in different ways. Athens became a great democracy (a form of government ruled by its people) and was governed by all the free males in the city. Sparta was a military state ruled by a small group of people. Athens became wealthy from its trade and colonies. The wealth of Sparta came from the work of slaves. There was great rivalry between Athens and Sparta, which eventually led to a war for rule of Greece in 431 B.C.

Athens

Athens became especially prosperous during the period from 500 to 430 B.C. This period is called the *Golden Age of Athens*. It is also known as the *Golden Age of Pericles* because *Pericles*, a famous politician and speaker, was able to influence government voting on various issues. One of his most important achievements was to organize the rebuilding of the Acropolis, a hill where a group of temples had been destroyed by the Persians. This included the Parthenon, one of the most famous buildings of ancient Greece.

The Golden Age of Athens was a time of great writing and learning. During this time, Athens became the center of Greek civilization and culture. Many great artists and thinkers came to Athens and thrived. Great architecture and sculpture was created and plays were performed in open-air theaters.

Philosophy also thrived during this era. Philosophy means the love of knowledge and wisdom. *Socrates* was a great Athenian philosopher. He was a teacher who asked his students careful questions. In order to answer these questions, the students would be forced to learn how to think. One of his students, *Plato*, wrote down the talks of Socrates and his pupils. Plato also became a teacher and a philosopher, and one of his most famous philosophy students was *Aristotle*. Artistotle was one of the first to look for the truth about things by testing facts and organizing ideas in a logical way. He was a scientist as well as a philosopher.

The Parthenon

Sparta

Sparta was a military state. Its soldiers became the most powerful in Greece and were known for their bravery. Every male Spartan had to become a soldier. Young boys left their homes when they were seven years old to begin their military training. They were taught to be loyal to the state and to obey orders. Men had to serve in the army until they were 60 years of age.

Spartan women were treated differently from Athenian women. They were citizens and were viewed as equals to men. Women did not become soldiers, but young girls had to stay physically fit and were trained in gymnastics, boxing, wrestling, and running. Women usually married by the age of 20 and were encouraged to have many children.

The Spartans conquered Messenia and made slaves of the people. The slaves were used to work the land and construct buildings. About 650 B.C., the slaves revolted. It took about 20 years for Sparta to regain total control.

Because of their emphasis on the military, Spartans did little in the arts and sciences. Today, when we use the word *Spartan*, we mean plain and uncomplaining. Spartans viewed the Athenian way of life with scorn. In 431 B.C., the Peloponnesian War broke out. Sparta defeated Athens after 27 years of war.

Athenians believed that everyone, both rich and poor, should be treated the same under the law. This was the beginning of *democracy*, a form of government in which the people rule.

The Assembly in Athens passed the laws. Every citizen of Athens was a member of the Assembly. This is an example of a *direct democracy*, where citizens participate directly in the government. (The United States has a *representative democracy*, where representatives are chosen to represent groups of people.)

Only free Athenian males could be citizens. A young man could take part in government when he was 18 years old by attending the Assembly. Women could not take part in government. Neither could males who were from other countries or who were slaves.

The Gods Of Olympus

Greek gods were important to the Greek way of life. The Greeks worshiped many gods and goddesses and invented stories, or myths, about them. Each god or goddess was a ruler of some part of nature or human life. Here are some of the gods and goddesses:

Zeus   The king of gods. He was the all-wise ruler of all the gods of the sacred mountain of Olympus (where the gods lived) and protected Greece. He was also the god of the sky and of thunder. The Olympic Games were held in his honor.

Athena   The daughter of Zeus and the patroness of Athens. She was the goddess of wisdom, courage, and victory. The Parthenon was built in her honor.

Apollo   The son of Zeus and twin brother of Artemis. He was the god of sun and light.

Hera   The sister and one of the wives of Zeus. She was the goddess of marriage and women.

Artemis   The twin sister of Apollo. She was the moon goddess and the protector of wild animals. Her arrows brought death.

Hermes   The messenger of the gods and the god of travelers and traders.

Poseidon   The brother of Zeus who ruled all the seas and rivers. It was thought that he caused earthquakes.

Aphrodite The goddess of love and beauty. She was the most beautiful of the goddesses and she protected lovers.

Ares   The god of war. He was hated by the other gods because of his violence.

Hestia   The goddess of the hearth. She was one of the most loved goddesses because she protected the city, home, and family. Every home had a shrine to her.

Hades   The brother of Zeus and god of the underworld. He ruled the kingdom of the dead.

Demeter   The goddess of agriculture, plants, and harvest. She caused changes in the seasons.

THE OLYMPICS

One of the great religious festivals in Greece was held in the town of Olympia in honor of Zeus. This festival lasted five days and featured competition in sports, music, and drama. It was held every four years. All wars stopped so that people from all over Greece could travel safely to Olympia. At the end of the games, oxen were sacrificed to Zeus, and everyone joined in a great feast.

The main event at the Olympic Games was the *pentathalon*. This competition included five different sports in which an athlete had to compete. It included a foot race, discus throwing, long jump, javelin throwing, and wrestling. The Olympic Games also included running, chariot races, horse races, and boxing matches.

Our modern Olympic Games are copied from this festival. They were started again after many centuries in A.D.1896 by a Frenchman named ***Baron Pierre de Coubertin***. In today's opening ceremony, an athlete lights the Olympic flame just as in 776 B.C., when an athlete first lit the fire on the altar where a sacrifice to Zeus was made.

Accomplishments of the Greeks

1 They developed the world's first democracy.

2 They were the first people to take a scientific approach to medicine by observing and carefully studying diseases. Hippocrates is known as the father of medicine.

3 Playwrights wrote and produced the first dramas in outdoor theaters. Euripides and Sophocles are two of the most famous playwrights.

4 They invented the rules of geometry as well as other mathematics. Euclid, a mathematician, wrote a geometry text called Elements. Only the Bible has been more widely studied.

5 They developed the art of philosophy to search for wisdom and truth. Three of the world's greatest philosophers were Socrates, Plato, and Aristotle.

6 They created outstanding literature and poetry. Two great poems, the Iliad and the Odyssey, told by Homer, are still read today. Sappho, a female poet, wrote beautiful love poems.

7 They wrote the first histories.

8 They studied and described a way to classify, or group, different types of plants.

9 They created magnificent buildings and beautiful sculpture. Greek architecture made heavy use of columns, which were decorated in different ways.

Greeks were also brillant architects. Among their many contributions to building are three styles of columns: Doric, Corinthian, and Ionic.

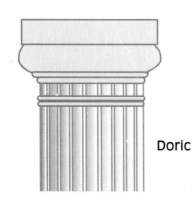
Doric

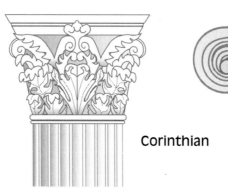
Corinthian

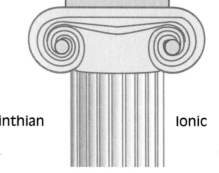
Ionic

Alexander the Great

King *Philip II of Macedonia* defeated the weakened city-states of Greece after the Peloponnesian War and became the ruler of all Greece. Philip united all the city-states of Greece and formed one country. He was murdered, but after his death, his son Alexander, who became known as *Alexander the Great*, took over. He was 20 years old at the time. By the time he was 22, in 334 B.C., he led his army into Persia and defeated King *Darius* (see page 8).

Alexander's empire was the largest in the ancient world. It stretched from Greece in the west to India in the east. Alexander spread Greek culture to many areas in his empire. He established great cities throughout, including Alexandria on the Nile in Egypt. Alexander wanted to unite all the peoples of his land, but he did not live to see his plan fulfilled. He died when he was only 32 years old.

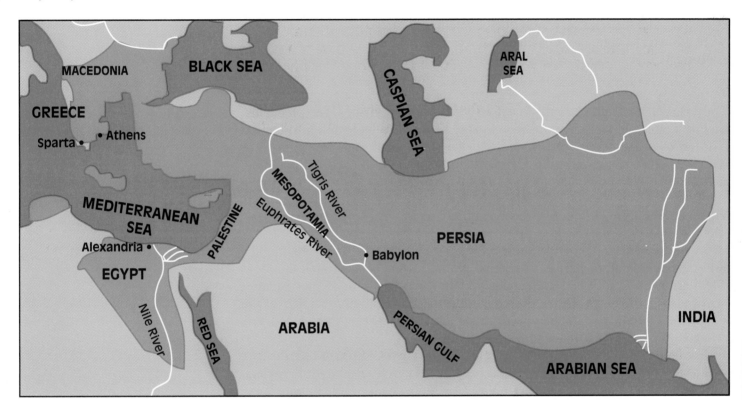

4 Ancient Rome

The city of Rome began as a small village in an area of seven hills on the Tiber River in southern Europe. The villages grew in the hills until they became one large town. This town eventually became the largest empire in the world, with hundreds of nationalities and tribes and almost 100 million people.

The Roman Republic

Around 750 B.C., a people called Etruscans invaded and conquered Rome. They ruled for about 200 years. Romans overthrew their king around 500 B.C. and drove out the Etruscans. The people of Rome set up a new form of government called a *republic*. A republic is a form of government where there is no king and the citizens choose the people to run the government. Free men were allowed to vote, but women and slaves were not.

Roman citizens were divided into two classes: The *patricians* were rich nobles and the *plebeians* were common people, such as farmers and workers. In the early years of the republic, the patricians controlled the government. Only patricians could enter the Senate where laws were made. The plebeians had little voice in the government and many of the laws were unfair to them.

After over a hundred years of struggle, the plebeians made a few gains. They won the right to have the laws written down and displayed in the public areas so that the laws could not be suddenly changed. They also gained the right to elect two officers, called *consuls*, to look after interests of the ordinary citizens. The Roman Republic lasted until 27 B.C., when Augustus became dictator.

By the second century B.C., Rome had become a powerful state. Its mighty army conquered all of Italy and eventually ruled all the lands around the Mediterranean Sea. It had even conquered the Greeks. Rome's chief enemy was Carthage in North Africa. Rome and Carthage fought three wars over the course of a hundred years; they were called the *Punic Wars*. They ended when Rome burned Carthage to the ground in 146 B.C.

The lands ruled by the Romans were called *provinces*. Roman provinces had to pay taxes to Rome. The capital became very rich. Rome itself became a city of the very rich and the very poor. Governing such a large empire was difficult, and the Romans began to turn to military leaders as rulers.

The Beginning of the Roman Empire

In 46 B.C., a great general and military hero named Julius Caesar took power in Rome. As the dictator, Caesar built new buildings, reduced taxes, and made life better for the plebeians. Julius Caesar was their hero. Because of his military leadership, soldiers were loyal to him. But the Senate, made up of patricians, thought he had too much power. So, in 44 B.C., some senators murdered him.

Caesar's adopted son, *Octavian*, took power in 27 B.C. He called himself *Augustus*, which means "great." Augustus became the first emperor of Rome. No longer a republic, this became the beginning of the Roman Empire. Augustus's rule began a 200-year period known as the *Pax Romana*, or the *Roman Peace*. It was mostly a time of peace and progress.

Augustus ruled from 27 B.C. to A.D. 14. He was a fair and able ruler and did many things for the Roman Empire: He maintained the peace, restored order in the army, established fair taxes, constructed many roads and buildings, and encouraged science, art, and literature.

Rome had a number of strong and able emperors who ruled for many years, expanding the territories and maintaining peace. With the death of *Marcus Aurelius*, in A.D. 180, a long decline began.

Julius Caesar

The Decline and Fall of Rome

The Roman Empire stretched from the Middle East to Great Britain. It was so large that Alexander the Great's empire was just an eastern province. Because of its vastness, it was hard to control. About A.D. 290, the emperor *Diocletian* divided the empire into two sections — the *Western Empire* and the *Eastern Empire*. Diocletian began the shift of power from Rome, the capital of the Western Empire, to the east. Once Emperor *Constantine* took over, in A.D. 324, he completed the shift, making Constantinople the main capital when the city was defeated in A.D. 330 (see pp. 38–39).

In the fifth century A.D., Germanic tribes and Mongol people called *Huns* invaded the Roman Empire. Romans referred to the Huns and Germanic tribes as *barbarians*, which then meant that they lived outside the empire. Eventually, the Huns conquered the Western Empire. The Eastern Empire survived for another thousand years.

Reasons for the Fall of Rome

 1 There was no orderly way of choosing an emperor. It was often done by military leaders, who chose soldiers rather than effective rulers. The military often murdered emperors whom they didn't like.

2 To support the large army, Romans were heavily taxed. This created burdens for common people.

3 Small farmers could not compete with large landowners, who used slaves for labor. Less food was grown because of poor farming methods on estates.

4 People without jobs, such as out-of-work small farmers, used up tax money.

5 Diseases killed about a third of the people.

The Roman Empire was attacked by barbarian tribes during the fifth century A.D.

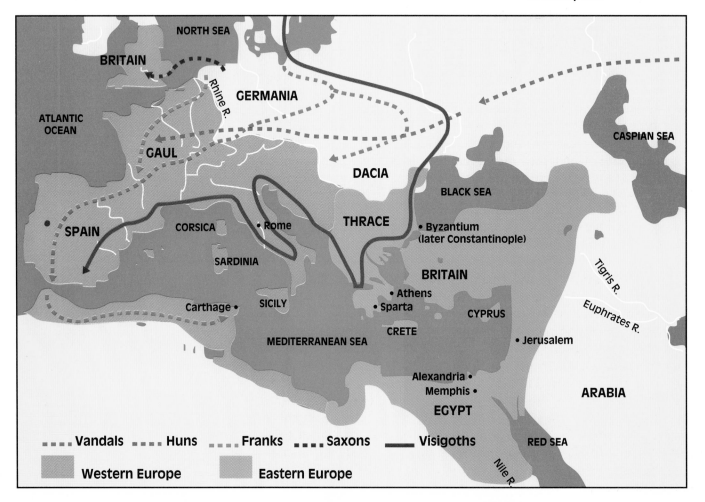

Legend:
`....` Vandals   `....` Huns   `....` Franks   `....` Saxons   `——` Visigoths

Western Europe   Eastern Europe

Map labels: NORTH SEA, BRITAIN, GERMANIA, Rhine R., ATLANTIC OCEAN, GAUL, DACIA, CASPIAN SEA, BLACK SEA, THRACE, Byzantium (later Constantinople), SPAIN, CORSICA, Rome, SARDINIA, BRITAIN, Tigris R., Athens, Sparta, CYPRUS, Euphrates R., Carthage, SICILY, CRETE, Jerusalem, MEDITERRANEAN SEA, Alexandria, Memphis, ARABIA, EGYPT, RED SEA, Nile R.

The Roman Gods

Roman gods were very much like Greek gods, but they had different names. Religion was the center of the Roman home and every family kept a shrine to the gods of the household— Janus and Vesta. Romans also built temples to their gods and goddesses.

Jupiter	**The king of gods and god of light.**
Juno	**The queen of the gods.**
Vesta	**The goddess of the hearth.**
Mars	**The god of war.**
Ceres	**The goddess of the harvest, mother of the earth.**
Minerva	**The goddess of wisdom.**
Venus	**The goddess of love. Her son was Cupid.**
Janus	**The god of the beginnings. The first month of the year, January, is named for him.**
Diana	**The goddess of the moon and of hunting.**
Neptune	**The god of the sea.**
Vulcan	**The god of fire.**
Mercury	**The messenger of the gods and protector of traders.**

The Beginnings of Christianity

During the reign of Augustus, a man named *Jesus* was born. He was a Jew who lived in Nazareth in the Roman province of Judea. Little is known about his childhood. All we know of Jesus comes from the Gospels of the New Testament in the Christian Bible. Jesus became a religious teacher with many followers. His followers called him the Christ, which means "the anointed one." Jesus taught people to love God and their neighbors as much as they loved themselves. This teaching stressed the importance of forgiving people, living an unselfish life, and being sorry for your sins. The religion built on the teachings of Jesus became known as Christianity. It took hold as the Roman Empire was falling apart.

Roman officials believed Jesus was dangerous. He was arrested and put to death by crucifixion (fastened to a cross until he died). Despite the death of Jesus, Christianity grew and spread all over the Roman Empire. A number of Roman emperors tried to crush the religion. They put Christians in jail and even murdered them. This cruel punishment lasted for many years until the emperor Constantine became a Christian in A.D. 312 and made Christianity legal. Three centuries after the death of Jesus, Christianity became the main religion in the empire.

Accomplishments of the Romans

1 They wrote a set of laws that became the basis of many legal systems for many countries of Europe and Latin America.

2 They built roads, bridges, and aqueducts to carry water. Built on the architecture developed by the Greeks, Roman architects built the arch, the dome, and the column. Some famous Roman buildings are the Temple of Vesta, the Pantheon, the Colosseum, the Theater of Pompey, and the Arch of Titus.

3 They created sculptures that actually looked like the people they portrayed, a first in ancient times.

4 Their language (Latin) became the basis for many other languages including, French, Italian, Spanish, and Portuguese.

5 The Roman poet Virgil wrote an epic poem, the Aeneid, which traces Rome's origins to Aeneas, one of the warriors in the Iliad by Homer (see p. 18).

6 They invented Roman numerals, which are still used today.

7 They united people and created peace in a vast empire.

Romans were excellent builders who incorporated arches, columns, and domes in their buildings. Even viaducts were designed using arches and columns.

THE SEVEN WONDERS OF THE ANCIENT WORLD

The Seven Wonders of the Ancient World are famous buildings and statues from ancient history. The list was made by a Greek writer over 2,000 years ago. Today, all have been destroyed or stand in ruins, except for the Egyptian pyramids.

The Colossus of Rhodes. A huge statue of the Greek god Apollo that stood in the harbor of Rhodes in Greece. An earthquake destroyed it.

The Great Pyramids of Egypt. The magnificent tombs for the kings of Egypt.

The Mausoleum. Mausolus was a king in Asia Minor. Upon his death, his wife built him a monumental tomb at Halicarnassus.

The Temple of Artemis. The Greeks built this temple to the goddess Artemis at Ephesus. It was burned to the ground by an invading army.

The Hanging Gardens of Babylon. King Nebuchadrezzar II built these magnificent gardens with terraces. Water had to be pumped up to the top.

The Pharos Lighthouse. A huge lighthouse that was built in Egypt by the Greeks.

The Statue of Zeus. A beautiful statue of Zeus made of marble, ivory, and gold stood at Olympia in Greece.

The Colossus of Rhodes

ASIA
(3000 B.C. – A.D. 1900)

1 Ancient India and China

Like Egypt along the Nile River and the Mesopotamian civilizations along the Tigris and Euphrates rivers, early civilizations of Asia began along great rivers. The Indus River of India and the Yellow River in China were where they began. Asia has seen the rise and fall of many developed civilizations and great empires. The sites of these ancient cultures have grown to be the most populated places on Earth.

India (3000 – 1500 B.C.)

India had one of the oldest civilizations. It began over 4,000 years ago, in an area known as the *Indus River Valley*. The main cities were Mohenjo-Daro and Harappa, and they were very much alike although they were 350 miles apart. Evidence of these ancient cities was found by archaeologists (people who study the life of ancient peoples) in the 1920s. They uncovered drainage and sewer systems, homes with bathrooms, large farms with irrigation canals, and many artifacts including jewelry, pottery, woven cloth, and tools and implements of copper and bronze.

What happened is a great mystery. Archaeologists are not sure, but a drought or flood may have wiped them out. Or, people may have scattered after an invasion. They were gone by 1500 B.C. The people who replaced them were nomads who herded animals. Hundreds of years went by before anyone built new cities in India.

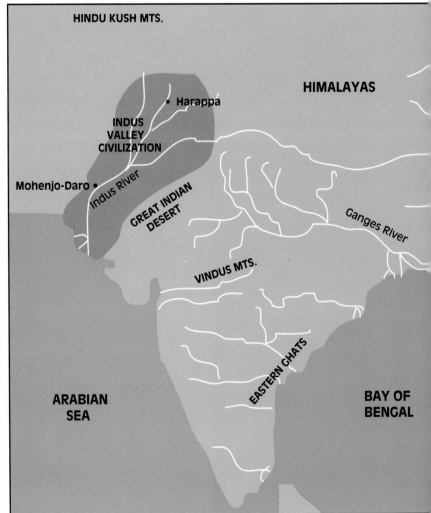

Indian civilization is believed to have begun in the Indus River Valley.

Hinduism

The nomadic people who entered northern India and the remaining scattered peoples of the Indus River cities formed a new culture in northern India. It was from this culture that the religion of Hinduism developed, beginning about 1500 B.C. Its special language was Sanskrit.

Hindus had thousands of gods and goddesses, and their priests sang from memory many long and complicated hymns to them. More than a thousand hymns were collected in the Hindu sacred text *Rig-Veda*.

Another sacred Hindu text, the *Upanishads*, was written about 400 B.C. In it, the basic ideas of Hinduism were collected:

- **Brahman is the one great spirit, or supreme being.**

- **The Self, or Soul, called Atman, is a part of Brahman.**

- **Nothing living ever truly dies, and the spirit passes from one living thing to another. This is called reincarnation.**

- **All Hindus must seek perfect understanding, called moksha. In moksha, the self disappears and becomes one with Brahman.**

The Caste System

Closely tied to Hinduism was the caste system. People divided into four main groups, or castes:

- **Priests (also called Brahmans) and scholars**

- **Warriors**

- **Merchants, farmers, and craftspeople**

- **Peasants and servants**

People who did not belong to any group were called *untouchables*, and they were the lowest group of all. Indian Nationalist leader Mohandas Gandhi called them *Harijan*, which means "children of God." The caste system was outlawed in India in 1950, but many people still mix only with people of their caste.

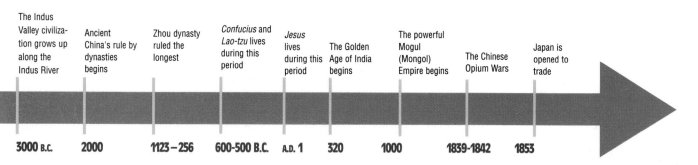

The Indus Valley civilization grows up along the Indus River	Ancient China's rule by dynasties begins	Zhou dynasty ruled the longest	*Confucius* and *Lao-tzu* lives during this period	*Jesus* lives during this period	The Golden Age of India begins	The powerful Mogul (Mongol) Empire begins	The Chinese Opium Wars	Japan is opened to trade
3000 B.C.	2000	1123 – 256	600-500 B.C.	A.D. 1	320	1000	1839-1842	1853

Buddhism

A young man named *Siddhārtha Gautama* was born near the Himalayas about 563 B.C. Just before he became 30 years old, he left his wife and son and went away to find the meaning of life. After fasting and disciplining himself harshly, he was not satisfied. Finally, he meditated deeply under a tree. When he finished, he believed that the truth had been made known to him. He gave his first sermon to the five wisdom seekers who had journeyed with him, and from then on was known as *Buddha*, or "the enlightened one." He taught that suffering is brought on by peoples' desires, and that suffering can be ended—and complete happiness found—by ending all desires.

Buddha taught his followers to treat all living things with loving kindness. Buddhism appealed to people because it rejected the caste system and treated everyone—women and men, rich and poor—with respect. It was taught in the everyday language of the people, not in Sanskrit.

Later, Buddhism spread to China and Japan but nearly died out in India.

Accomplishments of the Ancient Indians

1 **They founded the Hindu religion. Hinduism is one of the chief religions in India today.**

2 **They originated the Buddhist religion. Buddhism rejected the caste system promoted by Hinduism.**

3 **They further developed art and architecture, especially of temples.**

4 **They wrote fine literature, particularly in Sanskrit, including fables, stories, and poems. Sacred texts include the Rig-Veda.**

The Mauryan Empire

The Mauryan Empire, from 321 to 185 B.C., was the first to unite most of India under a central government. Its center was along the Ganges River and its capital was Pataliputra. Great rulers of the Mauryan Empire were *Chandragupta* and *Aśoka*.

Chandragupta came to power in 322 B.C. and ruled until 298 B.C. With his army of 70,000 soldiers, 9,000 elephants, and 10,000 chariots, he conquered northern and central India, as well as what is today western Pakistan and part of Afghanistan. He was a stern ruler, but his empire prospered.

Aśoka, the grandson of Chandragupta, ruled from 273 to 232 B.C. He guided India into a period of peace. A religious ruler, Aśoka sent missionaries into other countries to spread the message of Buddha. He also established hospitals, forbade animals as sacrifices, and urged vegetarianism. Aśoka was regarded as a kind and noble ruler.

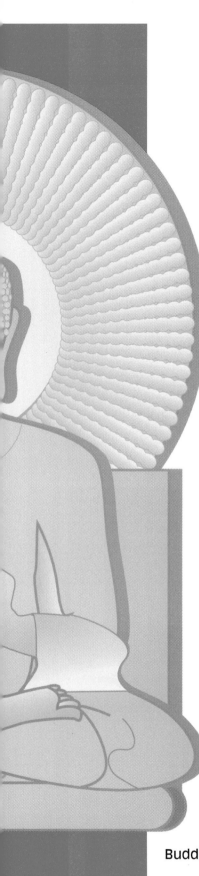

The Gupta Empire

Hundreds of years after the first Chandragupta died, another Indian ruler took his name. The Gupta Empire was begun by *Chandra Gupta I* in A.D. 320. He was the first of many rulers of his family who reigned over the empire until A.D. 500. The Guptas originally ruled a small kingdom in northeast India, but eventually their empire came to include all of northern India and parts of central and southern India. Like the Mauryan Empire before it, the capital was Pataliputra on the Ganges River.

After the Guptas took control, they restored law and order and people began to prosper again. The Gupta reign came to be known as the *Golden Age of India*.

Under the Gupta Empire, people followed both the Buddhist and Hindu religions (see pp. 27–28). The Gupta Empire ended when Muslim Turks invaded from Central Asia. The Golden Age of India had come to an end, and a new religion was brought to India.

Accomplishments during the Golden Age of India

1 Medical doctors set broken bones, used plastic surgery to repair ears and noses, and gave the first shots to prevent diseases.

2 Mathematicians invented the decimal (base-ten) number system and the Arabic numerals that are still in use today (1 to 9). They also developed the idea of zero and the concept of infinity, or endlessness, represented by the symbol ∞.

3 Great books and epics (stories told in long poems), such as the Mahabharata, Ramayana, and the Bhagavad Gita.

4 Artists, musicians, and dancers flourished. They developed classical dances and music still enjoyed today.

5 Textiles were created from slender threads, including cashmere, calico, and chintz.

Buddha from India

Muslim Influences upon India

- ❖ Government. Muslims became the ruling class over the more numerous Hindus.
- ❖ Religion. Islam grew in India and hostility between the Hindus and Muslims also increased. Muslims remained a distinctly separate group from the larger population of Hindus.
- ❖ Language. Arabic and Persian languages were introduced. Persian was the official language of the Mogul Empire. Over time, the Persian and Hindi languages formed into a new language, called Urdu.
- ❖ Architecture. Muslims built many palaces, mosques, and other monuments using arches and domes. Muslim architecture was much simpler than the ornate Hindu architecture.

Mogul (Mongol) Empire

Muslims began to invade India between A.D. 1000. and the 1500s. The Muslims were followers of a religion called *Islam*. Muslims believed that people were created equal, and that anyone can improve his or her social status by hard work. This was a very different belief from the one that put forth the Hindu caste system and caused many conflicts between Hindus and Muslims.

The word *Mogul* comes from the Persian-Indian word for Mongol. The Mogul Empire was founded in 1526 when *Babur*, the Mogul ruler of Afghanistan, conquered India and united it with Afghanistan.

The greatest Mogul leader was *Akbar*, whose name means "great." He was the grandson of Babur and only 13 years old when he became king in 1556. He ruled for 49 years, until 1605. Akbar expanded the empire's territories and provided a strong central government. During his rule, India became one of the leading centers of culture. Musicians, dancers, artists, and poets were invited to produce great works. Some of the most magnificent *mosques* (places of Muslim worship) were built during this period. This includes perhaps the most famous Indian monument, the Taj Mahal, built by *Shah Jahan* as a tomb for his wife. Akbar was also a just ruler who treated Hindus as equals of Muslims. He removed taxes on non-Muslims and forbade taking Hindus as slaves. He is considered one of history's finest rulers.

The last ruler of the Mogul Empire, *'Alam-gīr*, ruled from 1658 to 1707. He tried to force Hindus to become Muslims. He taxed non-Muslims and would not permit them to build Hindu temples. This led to many revolts. A group called the Rajputs successfully fought the Muslims and saved Hinduism in northern India. The kingdom became weak and broke into smaller states. Muslims had great influence upon India.

British Rule in India

The Portuguese explorer **Vasco da Gama** was probably the first European to reach India. Trade routes were soon established with England, France, and Denmark. In the 1600s, the British East India Company built trading posts in Calcutta, Bombay, and Madras. As the Mogul Empire weakened, the East India Company began controlling territories. By the late 1700s, Great Britain had become India's most powerful ruler, overthrowing Indian rebellions as well as the French, who tried to take control. The English gained complete control of India, and in 1877 announced Queen Victoria of England to be the Empress of India.

By the 1800s Britain was the world's largest *imperial* power. Imperialism exists when one country tries to extend its power and control over another. India became Britain's largest and most productive colony. For this reason, India was often called the Jewel in the Crown. The British made great profits from industries, such as textiles, in India, which they shipped back to England. As a result, however, the British destroyed India's own economy.

The British made a number of improvements in India. They stopped local wars, and built railroads, highways, hospitals, and a telegraph system. By developing industry, they created jobs. On the other hand, the population grew so fast that the demand for jobs could not be filled. Most Indians lived close to starvation, and paid high rents and taxes. The English lived far better than the Indians and kept themselves segregated (separated).

The Fight for Independence

Mohandas Gandhi

Eventually the Indians began to revolt. When the British passed laws in 1919 that forbade Indians to hold group meetings, 2,000 people, led by **Mohandas Gandhi**, gathered in a town square at Amritsar. British soldiers killed nearly 400 unarmed men, women, and children. Gandhi called for a nationwide nonviolent protest and urged Indians to refuse to obey the British. He called this *passive resistance*. His followers refused to buy British goods, to pay taxes, and to work for the government, and they disregarded British law. Gandhi was put in jail for two years, yet the independence movement still gained force. Finally, the British gave in and began to talk about granting India limited self-government. A long struggle for independence did not fully come until 1947, when the modern nations of India and Pakistan were formed. One of Gandhi's followers, **Jawaharlal Nehru**, became India's first prime minister, and India became the world's largest democracy.

China

Chinese civilization grew up along two large rivers. The first was called the Huang He, which means Yellow River. In the Yellow River Valley, people farmed rice, soybeans, barley, and wheat. Many villages were walled to protect them from invaders. Each of the small villages had its own government. The second river was the Chang Jiang, or Long River, in the southern part of China. It was so powerful that it cut deep gorges through the Asian mountains.

The Rule of Dynasties

Ancient China's history is divided into dynasties and dates back to 2000 B.C. A *dynasty* is a succession of rulers from the same family. The Chinese believed that their rulers were divinely selected. They called this process the *Mandate of Heaven*. The Chinese had eleven major dynasties before a revolution put an end to the last emperor in 1911.

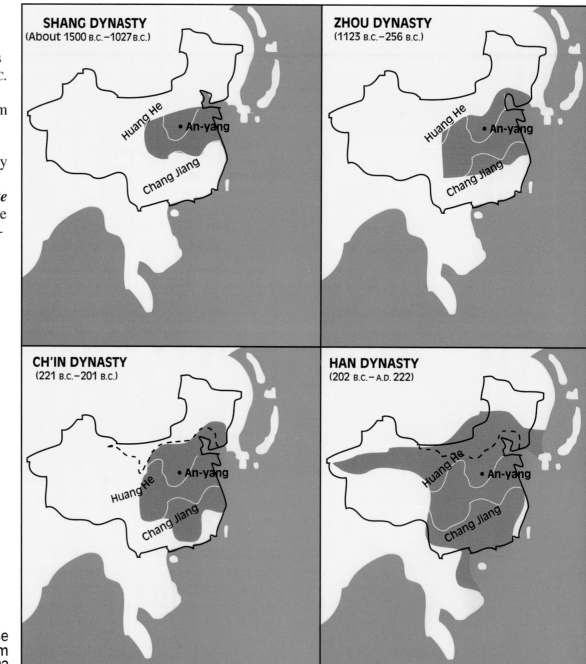

SHANG DYNASTY (About 1500 B.C.–1027 B.C.)

Huang He • An-yang Chang Jiang

ZHOU DYNASTY (1123 B.C.–256 B.C.)

Huang He • An-yang Chang Jiang

CH'IN DYNASTY (221 B.C.–201 B.C.)

Huang He • An-yang Chang Jiang

HAN DYNASTY (202 B.C.–A.D. 222)

Huang He • An-yang Chang Jiang

Major Chinese dynasties from 1500 B.C. to A.D. 222

The Teachings of Confucius

Confucius lived from 551 to 479 B.C. His teachings had great influence on the people of China. During his lifetime, he traveled all over China to instruct people about his ideas. He wanted to improve society and achieve good government. He taught that the following virtues are guidelines to a happy and useful life:

- **There were five relationships that needed to be obeyed: between ruler and subject, father and son, husband and wife, older brother and younger brother, friend and friend.**

- **Be sincere, polite, and unselfish.**

- **Obey and respect laws and traditions.**

- **Work hard and respect learning.**

Early Chinese Dynasties

DYNASTY	CULTURE	ART	RELIGION & PHILOSOPHY	FAMOUS LEADERS
HSIA 2000 – 1500 B.C.	millet and wheat cultivated potter's wheel used animals domesticated	black pottery		
SHANG 1500 – 1027 B.C.	writing invented silkworms cultivated for silk the wheel used on war chariots	white pottery fine bronze worked marble and ivory carved jade and turquoise used	belief in spirit world filial piety ancestor worship	
ZHOU 1123 – 256 B.C.	astronomy advanced crossbow invented	lacquer	Confucianism Taoism	
CH'IN 221 – 202 B.C.	Great Wall built		Legalism official policy	Ch'in Shih took title Huang Ti, meaning emperor
HAN 202 B.C. – A.D. 222	iron sword used soybean cultivated	wall painting sculpture	Confucianism official policy	

Later Chinese Dynasties

DYNASTY	CULTURE	ART	FAMOUS LEADERS
WARRING STATES A.D. 222–589			
SUI A.D. 589–618	Grand Canal built		Yang Ti. world
T'ANG A.D. 618–906	building of schools	golden age of poetry, literature, art, music	Wu Chao, first female emperor
SUNG A.D. 960–1279	inventions of magnetic compass, paper money, book printing	golden age of painting porcelain	
YUAN/MONGOL A.D. 1279–1368	increase in trade abroad use of gunpowder as a weapon		Genghis Khan Kublai Khan
MING A.D. 1368–1644	Forbidden City built *Yung-lo* Encyclopedia of Chinese writings Grand Fleet makes China an international naval power		Chu Yuan-Chang
MANCHU A.D. 1644–1911			Empress Dowager Tz'u-hsi

The Opium Wars (1839–1842)

Because the Chinese would not trade with Western nations, the British smuggled opium from India into China. Many Chinese became addicted to the illegal drug, which made them unable to work. The Chinese government tried to stop the trade of this habit-forming drug, but their laws were not obeyed. In 1839, Chinese troops destroyed millions of dollars' worth of British opium. This led to the Opium Wars and three years of fighting between China and England.

The British won easily, and in 1842 a peace treaty was signed. The Treaty of Nanking gave the island of Hong Kong, off the southern coast of China, to England. Another result of the treaty was the opening of five Chinese ports to foreign trade.

Taoism

Taoism comes from the word *Tao*, which means the Way, or the Path, to happiness. Its founder was Lao-tzu, a philosopher who lived during the time of Confucius but who believed people should lead simple and natural lives in harmony with nature. By understanding nature's way, people will achieve inner peace. The supposed author of the *Tao-te Ching*, Lao-tzu encouraged people to meditate (to think quietly) about nature's way, and to be content with what they had—not to reach for fame or fortune. He also believed that there should be no interference from government.

Empress Dowager

The Empress Dowager was the ruler of China from 1861 to her death in 1908. Her name was Tz'u-hsi. She became one of the most powerful women in the history of China. Though ruthless, she abolished the centuries-old practice of foot binding, a custom which left girls and women permanently crippled.

During her reign, foreigners were taking control over parts of China. The Chinese resented this and eventually, the Empress also supported the anti-foreigner rebels known as the Boxers. This secret society attacked foreigners in many parts of the country. In 1900, the Boxer rebellion reached its peak. Western nations and Japan banned together and defeated the Boxers. Tz'u-hsi was forced to flee Beijing, and China was forced to pay millions of dollars in damages, which put the nation in debt. Tz'u-hsi returned in 1902, though in 1911, a revolution led by Sun Yat-sen made China a republic. This ended 267 years of Manchu rule.

Mao Tse-tung

Attracted to the nationalist ideas of Sun Yat-sen, Mao Tse-tung joined the army when he was 18 and fought in the revolution that overthrew the Manchu dynasty in 1911. Several years later, while studying at Peking University, he came across the teachings of Karl Marx, and committed his life to the ideas of socialism. Eventually, he became the leader of the Communist revolution and then chairman of the People's Republic of China (P.R.C.) from 1949 to 1959. Mao remained chairman of the Communist party until his death in 1976.

Chinese calligraphy is read from top to bottom.

Japan

Very little is known of Japan's history before the sixth century A.D. because there were no written records. Historians believe that the earliest people, called *Jomon*, lived by fishing and hunting on Honshu Island between 8000 and 300 B.C. About 200 B.C., the Jomon were replaced by the *Yayoi*. The Yayoi cultivated rice and irrigated the land. The Japanese had now become farmers.

Around A.D. 200, invaders came from Korea. These people were the *Yamato*, and they ruled from A.D. 250 – 710. They introduced Korean and Chinese culture, including Buddhism. The ruler in 607 was *Prince Shōtoku Taishi*. He sent students to China, the most advanced civilization of the time, to study its culture. As a result, the Japanese borrowed many things from the Chinese, including language, arts, mathematics, architecture, and agricultural techniques.

The Heian Period (A.D. 794 – 1185)

In 794, *Emperor Kammu* made the city of Heian (present-day Kyoto) the capital of Japan. The city's name means "capital of peace and tranquillity." Kammu lost his power to the Fujiwara family in 858. They ruled Japan for 300 years. The Fujiwara era was a time of refinement and luxury and came to be known as the Heian Period. The arts flourished and writing and poetry became popular.

Two of the most important writers of this period were *Lady Murasaki Shikibu* and *Lady Sei Sonagan*. Lady Murasaki wrote *The Tale of Genji*, the world's first novel. The story was about the upper class of Japan.

The Rise of Shoguns in the Feudal Age

Landowners in the country had created large estates and ruled them according to their own sets of laws, rather than the emperor's. The lords, or landowners, were given land by small farmers who, in turn, received their lord's protection from other warring lords. The exchange of land in return for service or protection is called *feudalism*. The great lords were called *daimyo*. They hired lesser lords to fight for them, called *samurai*. The samurai warriors fought for the lords and had to be absolutely loyal to them. They lived by a code of behavior called *bushido*, or the "the way of the warrior." This was a strict code of absolute obedience. The samurai were rewarded with land and wealth, but were expected to die for their lords if necessary.

The central Heian government grew too weak to control the countryside. Two clans — the Taira and Minamoto — fought for control. The Minamoto took control. A military leader named *Yoritomo* led the new government. In 1192, Yoritomo was given the title *shogun*, which means "the emperor's general." The emperor remained at Kyoto, but the shogun Yoritomo ruled Japan. This system of government — in which Japan was ruled by military governments called *shogunates* — lasted for almost 800 years.

The major shogunates were: Kamakura Shogunate (1192 – 1333), Ashikaga Shogunate (1338 – 1573), and Tokugawa Shogunate (1600 – 1867).

Samurai armor is made of steel, silk, and bronze.

Isolation

Between 1200 and 1600, there were many civil wars. In 1600, when the *Tokugawa* shogunate came to power, it united Japan once again. In order to keep unity, the Tokugawa wanted all foreigners to leave Japan. In 1640, the shogunate expelled all foreigners, outlawed Christianity, and greatly reduced trade. No Japanese were allowed to leave the country. This began a period of isolation that lasted for 200 years.

Meiji Restoration (1868–1912)

Many Japanese were outraged over treaties the emperor made with Westerners. The samurai in southern Japan began attacking European ships and a full rebellion began. In 1867, the rebels overthrew the Tokugawa shogunate. In 1868, a 15-year-old prince was named emperor. He took the name *Meiji*, meaning "enlightened rule." This signified the return, or restoration, of the emperor's rule.

Meiji leaders began to Westernize, or adopt ways of Western countries of Europe and North America. They eliminated the positions of shogun, daimyo, and samurai. Students and officials were sent to Europe and America to study Western education, science, government, and military organization. The Japanese government built railroads, industries, and telegraph lines. In less than 35 years after the Meiji became emperor, Japan had built a modern, strong empire.

In 1853, Captain *Matthew Perry* of the United States came to Japan. Perry wanted a trade agreement. He brought four warships and a large force. This strong military show both impressed and frightened the Japanese. They gave Perry the trade treaty he wanted. Japan soon signed similar trade agreements with other Western nations. Isolation had been broken.

Matthew Perry

Accomplishments of the Early Japanese

1 Although they originally borrowed from the Chinese, the early Japanese gradually built their own culture. For example, Chinese language was adapted by the Japanese into a separate language.

2 They developed literature and poetry, including the writing of the world-famous novel The Tale of Genji.

3 They developed the Shinto religion, a form of nature worship. Ancestor worship also developed.

4 They placed great emphasis on good manners and a love of beauty.

THE BYZANTINE AND MUSLIM EMPIRES (A.D. 622–1932)

Ancient Middle East Roots

There were two great empires in the Middle East—the Christian Byzantine and the Muslim. Both were rivals for control of the Middle East. The Byzantine Empire thrived in present-day Turkey. The Muslim Empire centered on the Arabian Peninsula in present-day Saudi Arabia. Except for religion, these two empires had a great deal in common in their ways of life.

The Byzantine Empire

The Byzantine Empire was the Roman Empire of the east. One of Rome's great emperors was **Constantine**, who moved the capital of the Roman Empire to the city of Byzantium (see p. 21). He renamed the capital Constantinople (now Istanbul, Turkey), and it became the center of the Byzantine Empire. As the western half of Rome declined, the Byzantine Empire grew and became very wealthy from trade. Constantinople also became a great center of Christianity. Constantine had converted to the Christian faith and he encouraged Christian scholars to come and study.

Constantine

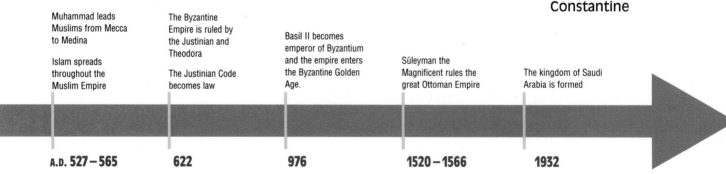

Muhammad leads Muslims from Mecca to Medina	The Byzantine Empire is ruled by the Justinian and Theodora	Basil II becomes emperor of Byzantium and the empire enters the Byzantine Golden Age.	Süleyman the Magnificent rules the great Ottoman Empire	The kingdom of Saudi Arabia is formed
Islam spreads throughout the Muslim Empire	The Justinian Code becomes law			
A.D. 527–565	622	976	1520–1566	1932

Justinian was a great army general and one of the greatest Byzantine emperors. Together with his wife, *Theodora*, he ruled from A.D. 527 to 565. Justinian expanded westward to recapture much of the Western Empire of Rome, including northern Africa, southern Spain, and Italy. He also instituted a new set of laws called the *Justinian Code*. These laws were based on the Roman laws. They were strict, but fair, and gave the same rights to everyone, rich or poor. This code of laws became a model for lawmakers all over western Europe.

In 976, *Basil II* became emperor. He expanded the empire and made it even more powerful and wealthy. The empire entered the *Byzantine Golden Age*. Artists, musicians, and architects thrived. Poets and historians wrote great works during this period. Education was stressed and new universities were built. Parks, playgrounds, museums, and libraries were built for the people. It was a time of great achievement.

The Byzantine Empire declined gradually from the 1000s to the 1400s, when it was constantly invaded by enemies. The Muslim Turks conquered Asian sections of the empire in 1071. Then Roman Catholics from western Europe began a series of wars called the *Crusades* (see also p. 74), eventually sacking the wealthy city of Constantinople in 1204. The Byzantine Empire ended in 1453 when the Ottoman Turks captured Constantinople.

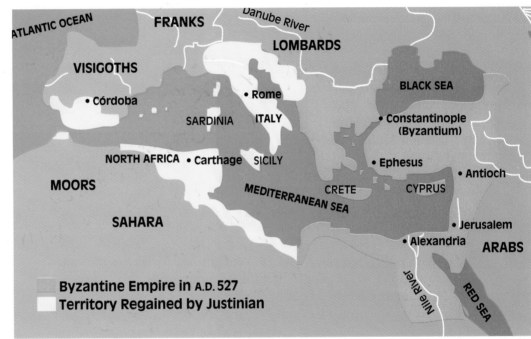

Byzantine Empire in A.D. 527
Territory Regained by Justinian

Accomplishments of the Byzantines

1 They helped preserve Greek and Roman culture by keeping alive the plays, poems, and ideas of the ancient Western world. The West (Europe) couldn't do this because during this time, most Europeans could not read.

2 They followed Roman laws, passing them on to western Europe.

3 They spread Christianity into eastern Europe, including Russia, Bulgaria, and Bosnia. Missionaries taught people how to read and write.

The Muslim Empire

By the eighth century, the Muslim Empire was the largest and most populated of its time. Its boundaries extended from India to Spain (see map). The first capital was at Damascus and later Baghdad. Its people were *Arabs*, who came from Arabia.

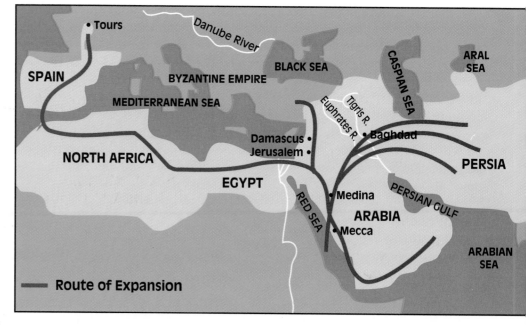

The Islamic religion of the Muslim Empire was founded by the prophet Muhammad in the seventh century. *Muhammad* was born in the city of Mecca in Arabia. He had a vision that he was to become God's messenger. He began to teach that there is only one God, called *Allah* (the Arabic word for God). Because many people thought Muhammad dangerous, he fled for his life to the city of Medina, where people accepted his teachings. Muhammad's flight is called the *Hegira*. The year of his flight, 622, is the first year of the Muslim calendar.

The Spread of Islam

In 630, Muhammad's army captured Mecca. Muhammad destroyed the statues of the other religions and set out to unify the peoples of Arabia. He conquered many other areas, and the Muslim Empire began to grow. Islam spread quickly. After Muhammad's death in 632, *Abū Bakr* convinced Muhammad's followers to continue his work. Abū Bakr became the first *caliph*, a religious leader and head of the Muslim state. His armies conquered the Persian Empire and much of the Byzantine Empire. Muslim armies then took North Africa and marched to the Atlantic Ocean. The Muslims did not force people to convert to Islam and allowed all religions to be practiced. However, Muslims paid lower taxes and were able to keep their land.

The *Umayyad* caliphs gained power in 661, after the murder of the fourth caliph, 'Alī. Muslims who supported 'Alī refused to recognize the Umayyad caliphs. This led to a revolt. Eventually, in 750, a new family of caliphs, called the *Abbasids*, took over. Their capital was *Baghdad*. The rule of the Abbasids lasted until 1055. During this time the greatest expansion of Islam took place. By the tenth century, Islam dominated a large part of the world.

The Muslim Empire gradually declined, and by the eleventh century the empire had been divided into a number of independent kingdoms. The family of *Seljuk* conquered the Abbasids and created their own empire. In 1258, the Mongols defeated the Seljuks. They were not Muslims and destroyed much of the Muslim culture. By 1453, the Ottoman Turks had established a new Muslim Empire that would last into the twentieth century.

Accomplishments of the Muslims

 1 They founded great universities, especially in Egypt, Baghdad, and Spain. They built many libraries and schools.

2 They brought the use of zero and Arabic numerals (adopted from India) to their empire. They also made advances in algebra and geometry.

 3 They used chemicals to make medicines, began performing surgery, and wrote medical textbooks, including the famous Book of Healing and the Canon of Medicine by Avicenna.

4 Astronomers kept records of the heavens and scientists studied the properties of light.

5 Great literary works, including the Rubáiyát by Omar Khayyám, were produced.

Islam is the religion based on the teachings of the prophet Muhammad. These teachings are written down in Islam's Holy Book, the *Koran* (also spelled *Qur'ān*). The Koran sets down five obligations to guide the lives of all Muslims. These five obligations are:

1. To confess that there is no God but Allah and Muhammad is His Prophet.

2. To pray five times a day.

3. To treat all Muslims as brothers and sisters and to give to the poor.

4. To not eat between sunrise and sunset in the holy month of Ramadan.

5. To make a pilgrimage to Mecca at least once, if possible.

Today there are two groups of Muslims. Sunni Muslims are the larger group. They believe that the only source of Islam is the Koran. The smaller group are called Shiite Muslims. They accept that there are three sources of Islam — the Koran, Muhammad, and 'Alī's descendants. They also believe that only the descendants of 'Alī can lawfully rule the Islamic community.

The Ottoman Empire

The founder of the Ottoman Empire was **Osman**. He was head of a Turkish group who called themselves Osmanlis, or "sons of Osman." These people later became known as Ottomans. Osman and his son, **Orkhan**, captured most of the Byzantine Empire. Orkhan was the first Ottoman leader to become a **sultan**, the Turkish name for emperor. Osman and his son were never able to capture Constantinople. In 1453, Sultan **Mehmet II** captured the city and rebuilt it. He ordered the Hagia Sophia, the largest Christian church, to be turned into a **mosque**, or Muslim place of worship. The former Christian capital now became the center of an Islamic empire.

By the sixteenth century, the Ottomans had enormous power under Sultan Süleyman I, also known as **Süleyman the Magnificent**, who ruled from 1520 to 1566. He greatly expanded the empire to include southern Russia and the Balkans and much of North Africa. The eastern lands extended to the Persian Gulf. During his rule, the Ottoman Empire reached its greatest heights in military power and culture. Süleyman reformed the educational and legal systems and encouraged the arts and sciences. Great mosques, schools, bridges, and monuments were built.

The military skill of the Ottomans was partly due to the drafting of Christians into a special army corps called the **Janissaries**. These hightly trained foot soldiers were rewarded with positions in the army and government.

The Ottoman Empire weakened greatly in the eighteenth and nineteenth centuries. In 1826, Sultan **Mahmud II** eliminated the Janissaries because they had so much power. He gradually westernized the empire. This did not stop the decline. A group called the **Young Turks** overthrew Sultan **Abdülhamid II** in 1909.

Janissaries could be recognized by their elaborate headdresses.

AFRICA (2000 B.C. – PRESENT)

1 The Kush

Kush was the land south of Egypt (see p. 10) in present-day Sudan. Its people, also called Kush, lived along the Nile River from about 2000 B.C. to A.D. 350. They were farmers and cattle raisers. They also mined gold and copper. The Kush were conquered and ruled by the Egyptians for thousands of years. The Egyptians went to Kush and took gold, ebony, ivory, cattle, and slaves back to Egypt. Many Egyptians came to live in Kush and the Kush began to worship the same gods. Their priests used Egyptian hieroglyphics to write.

When the Egyptian Empire weakened around 1100 B.C. , the Kush became independent. They built a great army and in 752 B.C. invaded and conquered Egypt. The Kush ruled Egypt for nearly a hundred years before they were conquered by the Assyrians (see p. 5).

After their defeat, the Kush moved their capital to Meroe. They realized they had lost Egypt because the Assyrians had iron weapons. The people of Meroe began to use iron. They made weapons and farm tools. Meroe became one of the biggest iron-making cities of the ancient world. It was from Kush that the knowledge of iron making spread south and west.

The Kush were defeated by the king and army of *Axum* in A.D. 350. After this, the Kush disappeared.

Leather, plant fiber, and wood are used to make this mask used in religious dances.

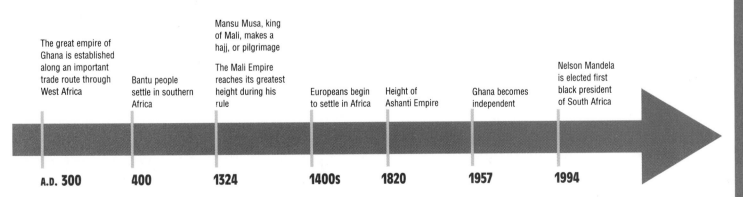

The great empire of Ghana is established along an important trade route through West Africa	Bantu people settle in southern Africa	Mansu Musa, king of Mali, makes a hajj, or pilgrimage The Mali Empire reaches its greatest height during his rule	Europeans begin to settle in Africa	Height of Ashanti Empire	Ghana becomes independent	Nelson Mandela is elected first black president of South Africa
A.D. 300	400	1324	1400s	1820	1957	1994

2 Early African Empires

Ghana

The first great empire in West Africa was that of the wealthy and mighty Ghana. The heart of the Ghanian Empire lay west of Kush, on the western edge of the vast grasslands of north-central Africa known as the Sudan. The *Soninkes* were among the first peoples to live in this region, from about A.D. 300 to 500.

The people of Ghana lived along an important trade route. To the south of Ghana was a large forest. To the north was the Sahara Desert. Ghana became a wealthy nation by controlling the roads and charging taxes for trade between the people of the forest and the people of the desert.

The people of the desert were called *Berbers*. They were traders who crossed the deserts in caravans, or large groups. The Berber traders exchanged salt and mined in the desert for gold. Later, Ghana also traded with Arabs who invaded North Africa.

Two metals played an important role in the development of Ghana—gold and iron. Ghana itself had little natural resources, but it became wealthy by controlling trade and acting as go-between for gold and salt that were exchanged in its territory. Iron was important because it allowed the people of Ghana to make and trade swords, daggers, arrows, and other weapons. This gave Ghana's warriors great advantage over their enemies, allowing them to easily conquer them.

The kingdom of Ghana first rose to power around the year 700 and disappeared around 1200. The capital city was Koumbi, and it had around 15,000 people. Koumbi was conquered and destroyed in 1076 by Berber Muslims known as *Almoravids*. They built a great empire in northwest African and northern Spain.

Other invaders attacked Ghana as well. The Arab Muslims tried to force the Ghanians to convert to their religion many times. In 1203, Ghana was attacked by the *Sosso* tribe. After that, Ghana became weak and powerless.

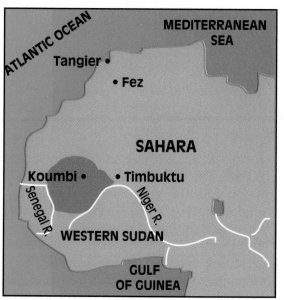

Gold, iron, and important trade routes brought about the rise of Ghana in the area of West Africa known as the Sudan.

Accomplishments of the Ghanians

1 They established important trade routes.

2 They controlled the gold and salt trade.

3 They controlled roads and charged taxes for passage, creating a wealthy nation.

Mali

Mali succeeded Ghana as the major kingdom in the western Sudan. The empire of Mali contained the former Ghana as well as much more territory.

The power shift began when **Sumanguru**, the leader of the Sosso tribe, destroyed Ghana in 1203. There was a power struggle between the Sosso and the **Mandingo** people, led by **Sundiata**. The Mandingo defeated the Sosso in 1235 and went on to found the Mali Empire. There is a legend that tells of Sumanguru vanishing during the battle and a giant baobab tree springing up at the spot. Descendants still claim Sundiata as their great national hero.

The capital of Mali was Kangaba on the Niger River. After Sundiata defeated Sumanguru, he moved the capital to Niani. Islam was the major religion. The kingdom of Mali became a key region in the Islamic world of the Middle Ages. The rulers were called **mansa**, which means "emperor" or "sultan." **Mansa Musa**, a descendent of Sundiata, was the most famous ruler in the history of the western Sudan. He became mansa in 1307 and ruled for 25 years. Mansa Musa extended the boundaries of his empire, promoted trade and commerce, and encouraged the spread of learning. He also loved the arts, including paintings, architecture, and literature. He was devoutly religious.

Mansa Musa made a pilgrimage to Mecca, the holy city of Islam. Such a pilgrimage is called a **hajj**, and is part of the five basic observances of the Islamic religion (see p. 41). Mansa Musa's pilgrimage was one of the grandest of all times. He spread his wealth throughout the cities he passed. Mansa Musa became famous and many people traveled to his kingdom. He died in 1332.

Mali maintained an enormous army to keep peace within its empire, believed to have been over 100,000 men. Mali's main crops were sorghum, rice, taro, yams, beans, cotton, and onions. People raised poultry, cattle, sheep, and goats. Mali replaced Ghana as the greatest power of the western Sudan, taking over the trans-Saharan gold/salt trade.

The Mali Empire was at its largest under Mansa Musa's rule, but after his death, the empire began to decline. By the end of the fifteenth century, it had dwindled to a small, unimportant state.

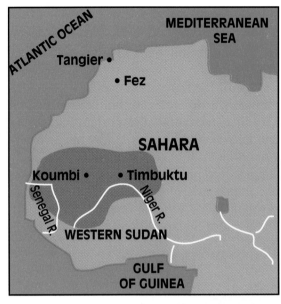

The Mali Empire rose with the decline of the Ghanians in the Sudan.

Accomplishments of the Malians

1 They established trade and commerce throughout their empire.

2 They promoted learning and education.

3 They received fame through Mansa Musa's hajj.

The Songhai

The Songhai resisted the rule of the Mali and built their own empire about the mid-1400s. They were river people who lived along the Niger. Gao was their capital. Another great city was Timbuktu, which became a great center of Islamic learning and a large trading center, with over 50,000 people.

The earliest Songhai were mainly farmers and fishermen. They first settled in a town called Kukya, which became their capital. Around the eighth century, the Berber nomads captured Kukya and the Songhai moved further north in a new town that became Gao. By the eleventh century, the leader of Songhai had converted to Islam. For the next 300 years, the Songhai were constantly trying to remain free of Mali rule.

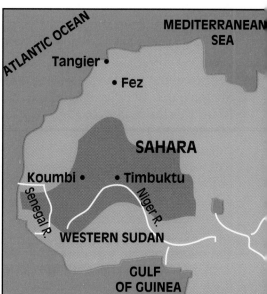

One of the fiercest warrior kings was *Sunni Ali Ber*. He came to the throne in 1464, recapturing the city of Timbuktu and later capturing the city of Jenne, another important trading center. Many thought him cruel, but he was highly regarded by his own people. Sunni Ali Ber was an able ruler with talent for organization and government. He divided his empire into provinces and placed governors in control. He understood the importance of the Niger River in commerce and in military operations. Around 1475, Songhai replaced its rival, Mali, as the dominant power in the western Sudan. Sunni Ali Ber died in 1492 after ruling for nearly 28 years.

Accomplishments of the Songhai

1 They established a great center of Islamic learning in the empire.

2 They encouraged skilled craftspeople and artisans.

3 They built and maintained a large army.

The Songhai Empire was established after the Mali Empire declined. The Songhai built a great center for trade and Islamic learning at Timbuktu, in the heart of the salt caravan routes from the Sahara to the Atlantic coast.

The Zanj

The people of Zanj lived on the eastern coast of Africa, from present-day Mozambique to Kenya, and including the island of Madagascar. They were mostly traders, exchanging ivory for wheat, rice, sesame oil, cotton, and honey. They also exported gold, tortoise shells, and slaves. The Zanj had been trading with China, Arabia, and India for almost 2,000 years when the Portuguese discovered them in the late 1400s. Between 1200 and 1500, trade with China, their farthest commercial partner, was extensive.

The people of Zanj built beautiful towns and were very good craftspeople. When the Portuguese arrived, they looted, destroyed towns, and killed citizens. Ruins and pottery fragments are the only things that exist from this lost kingdom.

Accomplishments of the Zanj

1 They established trade farther from home than any other African peoples.

2 They were skilled craftspeople and builders.

The Dogon people have lived in Mali since the 12th century.

Zimbabwe

A number of **Bantu** peoples (speakers of the ancient language of Bantu) moved from West Africa to the area between the Zambezi and Limpopo rivers in southern Africa. Beginning around A.D. 400, they began mining for gold in the hills around the rivers. They took the gold to the Indian Ocean where they traded it for cloth, glass beads, and other goods. Around 1100, one group of these people began constructing thick stone-walled buildings. The area encompassing these buildings became the capital of an important kingdom called Zimbabwe. Zimbabwe means "stone houses."

The builders of Zimbabwe were very skillful. The structures they built were sturdier and higher than those of other kingdoms. Neither mortar nor square corners were used, yet the stones fit together perfectly. They built a great stone city.

Zimbabwe became wealthy from its gold and ivory trade. The people were ruled by kings and were protected by a powerful army. Their empire lasted until the 1800s, when the last king was killed. Enemies destoyed the great buildings, and today only ruins remain. The current nation called Zimbabwe does not include the ancient ruins within its borders. It is a new and different country that chose the name **Zimbabwe** when it became independent from Great Britain in 1980.

Accomplishments of the Zimbabweans

1 They mined gold for trade and established a large gold and ivory trade.

2 They were excellent builders, especially of stone.

Even without mortar, these 800-foot granite walls at Zimbabwe stand 32 feet high.

3 The European Colonization of Africa

In the mid-1400s, the Portuguese began sailing from the Iberian Peninsula of Europe to the west coast of Africa. Prince **Henry the Navigator** encouraged the establishment of a number of trading posts along the west coast. The Portuguese were followed by the Dutch in the seventeenth century. During the 1800s, other Europeans moved into Africa. They took control of the continent, sometimes by force, and set up colonies. This became known as **colonial rule**.

The Industrial Revolution (see p. 88 – 89) had given Europeans the ability to make weapons that were better than any made in Africa. Inventions such as the steam engine, the telegraph, and the railroad gave Europeans the means to build empires. Europeans saw these developments as proof that they had the right to rule people who were not industrialized. They were often convinced that it was their duty as Christians to spread their religion, too.

Ten percent of the African continent was under direct European control by 1880, and by 1920 most of Africa was ruled by six European powers — France, Great Britain, Portugal, Germany, Belgium, and Italy. These were the major areas they settled and controlled:

France	**Algeria, Tunisia, French West Africa, Equatorial Africa, Madagascar**
Great Britian	**South Africa, Uganda, Kenya, Rhodesia, Egypt, Sudan**
Portugal	**Angola, Guinea, Mozambique, and the islands of Cape Verde, Sáo Tomé, Principe, Madeira**
Germany	**Tanganyika, South West Africa (Namibia), Togoland, Cameroon**
Belgium	**Congo**
Italy	**Somaliland, Eritrea, Libya**

Europeans wanted colonies that could supply raw materials for industries at home. There was a scramble for land. Each European country was afraid that the other countries would keep trade for themselves. African countries that would not sign trade agreements were taken by force. Many were tricked into signing agreements that they did not understand. By 1914, only Ethiopia retained its independence.

Some Africans resisted the invasion of their territory, but most were defeated. Peoples who at first accepted European rule became disillusioned. Many felt cheated and sought revenge, which often led to resistance and wars.

Africans tried to win back their freedom and some succeeded. Most, however, did not gain independence until the 1950s. European empires in Africa finally came to an end in the 1970s, when Portugal gave up large territories there, and in 1980, when Great Britain gave up colonial control of Zimbabwe.

Africa today

The Ashanti

The Ashanti lived in a tropical rain forest along the coast of the Gulf of Guinea in what is now called Ghana. They were farmers, hunters, and gatherers, and they mined gold. Many of these goods were traded with the people of the northern savanna country. Later, the Ashanti, like other nations, also became involved in slave trade. The desire to control this trade with the Europeans led to many conflicts among other African peoples.

In the late 1600s, *Osei Tutu*, a local Ashanti chief, convinced other clan chiefs to join in a military union. The chiefs agreed and together they defeated their rivals, the *Denkyira*. Tutu was then declared the leader of the newly formed Ashanti nation. The Ashanti Empire lasted for over 200 years, until the late 1880s, and was one of the larger empires in West Africa. In 1901, the British overran the government and made the Ashanti kingdom part of Great Britain's Gold Coast colony.

The African Slave Trade

The Portuguese first brought Africans to Europe as slaves in 1441. The plague (see p. 76) had killed many Europeans, and there were not enough workers. The slaves were sold for high prices. Over the next 60 years, the Portuguese enslaved 50,000 Africans, mostly from West Africa.

When European countries opened colonies in North, South, and Central America, the demand for slaves increased. European colonists did not want to do the heavy labor required to mine gold and silver or work the sugar plantations. Diseases from Europe had killed many of the Native Americans that the colonists had hoped would do the work. Some 10 million Africans were sold as slaves in the Americas over 350 years. It is thought that at least one out of three Africans brought to America died either as a result of the journey or from bad treatment.

Africans were brought to the Americas on board crowded slave ships. Many died on these ships and others became too ill to be sold at auction upon their arrival in the Americas.

5 Egyptians Rule Egypt

In 1805, *Muhammad Ali*, an Albanian-born Turkish army officer, became ruler of Egypt. He expanded Egypt's power up the Nile by controlling the river. He built a strong army and conquered the Sudan. In addition, he wanted to make his country a modern state, and asked the Europeans for help. After his death, Egypt's rulers continued Ali's plans, but they were not as successful. The British soon took control of the Suez Canal, which linked the Mediterranean and Red seas. By 1882, the British had taken control of all Egypt.

In 1922, Egypt gained limited independence. The British agreed to leave the country by 1936 except in the canal area, but World War II caused them to stay longer. Egyptians were tired of foreign control and wanted to be rid of it. Most Egyptians thought *King Farouk*, leader of the time, to be part of the problem. In 1952, the government was overthrown by a group of army officers led by *Gamal Abdel Nasser*. Nasser became the first Egyptian to rule Egypt after more than a thousand years of foreign control.

Gamal Abdel Nasser

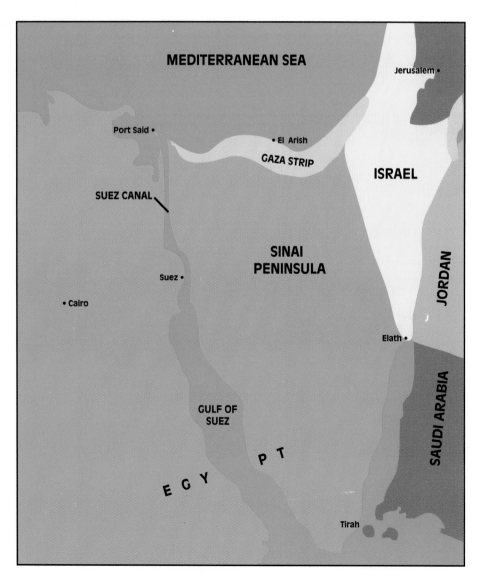

The 107-mile Suez Canal links the Mediterranean and Red Seas, and allows boats passage from Europe to Asia without navigating around Africa.

South Africa

South Africa was orginally inhabited by people called the *San*. They lived in the dry western part and hunted big game animals and gathered fruits and nuts. The San moved constantly, following food sources, and never built permanent homes.

Another people, called the *Khoikhoi*, lived near the San. They herded cattle and sheep as well as hunted and gathered. The San and the Khoikhoi are often referred to together as the *Khoisan*.

The eastern part of South Africa was occupied by groups of people who spoke Bantu languages. They farmed, raised livestock, and mined ore to make tools and weapons. The Bantu-speaking peoples made permanent homes and stayed in one place.

Bartolomeu Dias was a Portuguese sailor who sailed around the southern tip of Africa in 1488. He called it the Cape of Good Hope.

Around the mid-1600s, Dutch people begin settling the southern tip of Africa. Their settlement was called Cape Colony. The Khoisan fought for their land but were defeated and forced to work for the Dutch. More Europeans came and began to called themselves *Afrikaners*. The British called them *Boer*, which means "farmer" in Dutch. The mix of languages, particularly influenced by Dutch, was eventually called *Afrikaans*.

In the early nineteenth century, the British took over Cape Colony from the Dutch. English became the main language and all slaves were freed. This angered the Afrikaner settlers, so they decided to search for new lands. Their migration became known as the *Great Trek* (journey).

The Great Trek lasted for many years (1835–1840s) as the Afrikaners moved into the Bantu lands to the east and the north. They fought many battles, and most of the Bantu-speaking people lost their land. By 1854, the Afrikaners had won control and created two Afrikaner republics — the Transvaal and the Orange Free State. Slavery was abolished, but only white men could vote in these republics.

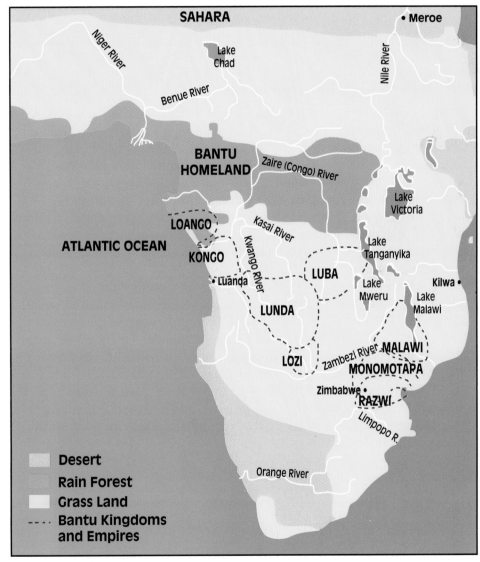

Desert
Rain Forest
Grass Land
- - - **Bantu Kingdoms and Empires**

The British and the Afrikaners continued to fight over who should control the government, in part because of the discovery of diamond and gold mines in the area. In 1899, war broke out between the two and lasted until 1902. It was called the **South African War** (also called the **Boer War**) and ended with the British defeating the Afrikaners. The republics were joined and, in 1910, they formed the Union of South Africa. **Louis Botha**, a former Afrikaner general, became prime minister of an all-white government.

APARTHEID

South Africa became even more of a white man's land after the formation of the new union. The blacks living there were limited in many ways. The best jobs went to whites, and it was difficult for blacks to buy or rent land outside areas set aside for them. In 1948, the South African government instituted a policy called apartheid. This was a policy of separation by race—white, colored, Asian, or African (Bantu or other). Whites were defined as Europeans, coloreds as mixed races, Asians as people from India, and Bantu as black Africans.

Nelson Mandela

Apartheid forced people into white and nonwhite racial groups. This separation is called **segregation**. There were separate restaurants, restrooms, drinking fountains, and beaches. Marriage was banned between races, and whites and blacks had to live in separate areas. Often the areas designated for blacks to live in, called townships, were small and overcrowded. Much of the housing was nothing more than shacks with no electricity.

The **African National Congress (ANC)** was a group formed to protest the whites' unfair treatment of blacks. Protests became violent in the 1960s when white police shot into groups of blacks protesting in the streets.

One of the leaders of the ANC was **Nelson Mandela**. He fought for a democratic and free society in which all people are equal. In 1964, he was arrested and charged with attempting to overthrow the government. An all-white jury found him guilty. Mandela served 27 years in jail and was released in 1990 by **F. W. De Klerk**, president of South Africa. De Klerk and Mandela worked together to run the government. In 1993, both Mandela and De Klerk won the Nobel Peace Prize for their efforts. In 1994, Mandela was elected president of South Africa.

THE AMERICAS (1200 B.C. – A.D. 1920)

1 Mesoamerica

The first advanced civilizations in the western hemisphere originated in the area called **Mesoamerica**, the region that is now Mexico and Central America, and around the western coast of South America. In these areas, several advanced civilizations developed, similar to those found in other parts of the world. Their chief crop was corn. Textiles, pottery, and jewelry of gold and silver were produced. There were city centers with canals and gardens, temples, and pyramids. Priest-emperors ruled and built armies, courts, and schools. Little is known about them because many of their written records were destroyed before their language could be understood by Europeans.

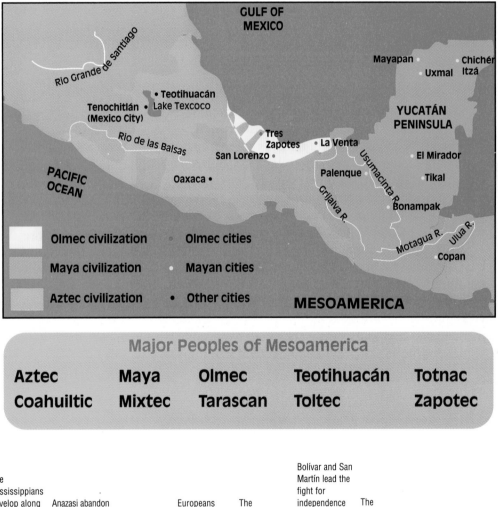

GULF OF MEXICO

Rio Grande de Santiago

• Teotihuacán
Tenochtitlán • Lake Texcoco
(Mexico City)

Rio de las Balsas

PACIFIC OCEAN

Oaxaca •

Mayapan   Chichén Itzá
Uxmal

YUCATÁN PENINSULA

• Tres Zapotes   • La Venta
San Lorenzo •

El Mirador
Palenque   Tikal
Usumacinta R.
Grijalva R.   • Bonampak

Motagua R.   Ulua R.
Copan

	Olmec civilization	•	Olmec cities
	Maya civilization	•	Mayan cities
	Aztec civilization	•	Other cities

MESOAMERICA

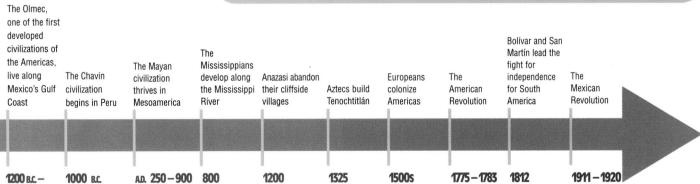

Major Peoples of Mesoamerica

| Aztec | Maya | Olmec | Teotihuacán | Totnac |
| Coahuiltic | Mixtec | Tarascan | Toltec | Zapotec |

The Olmec, one of the first developed civilizations of the Americas, live along Mexico's Gulf Coast

The Chavin civilization begins in Peru

The Mayan civilization thrives in Mesoamerica

The Mississippians develop along the Mississippi River

Anazasi abandon their cliffside villages

Aztecs build Tenochtitlán

Europeans colonize Americas

The American Revolution

Bolívar and San Martín lead the fight for independence for South America

The Mexican Revolution

1200 B.C.– A.D. 400   1000 B.C.   A.D. 250–900   800   1200   1325   1500s   1775–1783   1812   1911–1920

The Olmec

One of the first developed civilizations was that of the Olmec. They lived along Mexico's Gulf Coast between 1200 and 400 B.C. They were farmers and lived in thatched huts. The Olmec were a religious people ruled by priests. They built large temples, monuments, and pyramids to glorify their leaders. The Olmec are known for their great carved heads of stone, thought to be of Olmec rulers. More than 16 have been uncovered.

The Olmec developed the first calendar in the Americas. They also developed a counting system. Because of these and other achievements in art and politics, the Olmec were a great influence on later civilizations.

The Olmec civilization flourished for about 800 years, then disappeared.

Cobata is the largest of the Olmec carved heads, standing 11 feet high; it was carved between 1200 and 900 B.C.

Maya

The Maya built one of the most highly developed civilizations of Mesoamerica. They flourished between A.D. 250 and 900 in and around the Yucatán Peninsula (present-day southern Mexico, Belize, Guatemala, Honduras, and western El Salvador).

Most of the Maya were farmers who grew corn, squash, and cotton. They built at least 80 cities for trade, the largest of which was Tikal. The Maya were ruled by a noble class. Only people in this class could serve in the government or become priests. The king was the chief ruler and thought to have godlike qualities. Priests conducted the religious cermonies. They were held in high regard because every part of Mayan life had some kind of religious connection.

The Maya developed a system of writing and a calendar and were skilled in mathematics and astronomy. They built extraordinary monuments and buildings, some of which they decorated with wall paintings.

MAYAN GODS

Itzamna	The god of creation. The name means "lizard house."
Ix Chel	Moon goddess, patroness of weaving, medicine, and childbirth.
Kukulcan	A feathered serpent considered to be the god of kings.

Accomplishments of the Maya

1 They developed two calendars and a way to calculate time. The solar calendar had 365 days and was used for seasonal planting. The other was a 260-day festival calendar used for religious ceremonies.

2 They developed a mathematical system that included zero.

3 They developed a good knowledge of astronomy through careful observation of the sun, moon, stars, and planets.

4 They developed a writing system of symbols, or glyphs, the most complex in America.

5 They built 200-foot-high pyramids and elaborate temples, made pottery, and carved ornaments from jade.

The Aztec

The Aztec originally settled on Lake Texcoco in the early 1200s. After 200 years of constant warring, they conquered all the neighboring peoples. By the time the Spanish arrived in the 1500s, the Aztecs ruled a mighty empire in central and southern Mexico.

The capital of the Aztec Empire and the center of Aztec life was the city of Tenochtitlán (near modern Mexico City). The engineering skills of the Aztecs provided roads, raised channels to carry fresh water, and constructed dikes for irrigating the gardens throughout the city. Tlatelolco, the large marketplace in the capital, was a crossroads for trade where people came from all over to exchange goods.

The Aztec society was highly organized. There was one ruler, or emperor. Nobles ruled cities and served as judges. Priests performed religious duties, and the common people made up the majority of the population.

Religion was very important to the Aztecs. Magnificent temples and pyramids were built to honor the gods. The chief god was *Huitzilopochtli*, the god of sun and war. The Aztecs believed he needed regular human sacrifices in order to remain strong. Prisoners and slaves were used as victims, but sometimes the Aztecs' own people were chosen. To be sacrificed was an honor and believed to grant eternal life.

THE MAIN AZTEC GODS

Name	Domain
Huitzilopochtli	God of war and god of the sun.
Tezcatlipoca	The most powerful god, associated with destiny or fate.
Quetzalcoatl	The feathered serpent, god of learning and priesthood.

Quetzal bird

The Spanish Conquer the Aztecs

In 1519, a Spaniard named *Hernán Cortés* (see p .66) and 500 soldiers marched into Tenochtitlán looking for gold. The Aztec emperor *Montezuma* gave them gold and other gifts. The Spanish took Montezuma prisoner and overtook the city with their guns, horses, and canons — things the Aztecs had never seen before. There were numerous battles between the Aztecs and the Spanish. Many of the conquered people sided with the Spanish and the Spanish won. The Spaniards destroyed a great deal of the city to put up their own buildings. The new city was called Mexico City.

The Andean Civilizations

Another civilization developed along the western coast of South America in present-day Peru. These people lived in and around the Andes Mountains.

The Chavin

The Chavin were one of the earliest cultures to develop in South America. They lived in northern Peru from about 1000 to 200 B.C. At Chavin de Huantar, the center of their culture, the Chavin built a magnificent temple. The Chavin developed excellent stone carvings and fine pottery and ceramics. Some of the oldest gold work has been found among their ruins.

The Moche

The Moche civilization developed along the Moche River in northern Peru from about A.D. 200 to 800. Its people built grand pyramids, including the **Temple of the Sun**, a terraced pyramid made entirely of **adobe** bricks (adobe is a mixture of mud and straw that is baked hard by the sun). During an archaeological dig in 1987, the tombs of Moche rulers were discovered filled with gold and copper ornaments set with jewels. It proved that the Moche were among the greatest artisans of the ancient world.

The fortress city of Machu Picchu covers an area of five square miles and was built on a series of terraces carved into the side of a mountain more than 2,000 feet above sea level.

The Inca

The Inca is the most famous of the Andean civilizations. The Inca Empire began to develop about the same time as the Aztec Empire, and was at its most powerful in the late fifteenth century. It was the largest empire of its time, stretching about 3,000 miles along the coast of South America in the Andes Mountains. Its population was about six million people. (England had about 4 million people at the same time). The capital was Cuzco.

Accomplishments of the Incas

1 They developed the Quechua language (but no real system of writing).

2 They developed a method of counting and keeping records using quipu, a process of tying knots in strings. Using this method, they took a census and collected taxes.

3 They were highly skilled builders who cut stones by hand and built without the use of mortar. The stones were placed so tight that many buildings are still standing today. They also built a great network of stone roads, covering more than 15,000 miles.

4 They produced many beautiful works of art, including weavings and skilled metal workings.

The Rise and Fall of the Inca Empire

Two great rulers expanded the Inca Empire. *Pachacutec*, the ninth Inca emperor, was the first. *Topa*, his son, was the second. The Inca were at their most powerful during the reigns of those leaders, from 1438 to 1493. They united the people of the Andean region to form one great empire by forcing their government, law, religion, and language on the people they conquered.

After Topa died, the government became weak and civil wars began to break out. At about this time, *Francisco Pizarro* and his Spanish soldiers invaded the empire. They took the ruler, *Atahuallpa*, prisoner and killed him. The Spanish took over the Inca Empire, and it became part of the Spanish Empire.

② North America

Native Americans lived in North America as early as 9000 B.C. Many lived in southeastern Canada and east of the Mississippi in the United States. They hunted the deciduous forests and gathered roots and berries in the open country. Native Americans that settled in the West were also hunters.

The Adena

An advanced group of Native Americans lived in southern Ohio, Indiana, Kentucky, and West Virginia. They were called the Adena and they thrived about 1000 B.C. They built large mounds of earth to cover the tombs of their rulers. Their people raised corn, squash, and beans. The Adena were also skilled at making pottery.

These *Mound Builders* were skilled at farming and crafts and influenced the *Hopewell* people, who flourished mostly in southern Ohio and the Mississippi River valleys about 200 B.C. to A.D. 400. The Hopewell centers were in present-day Illinois, with smaller centers in Kansas City and other places along the Mississippi River. The Hopewell were also Mound Builders. Their mounds were large and rectangular, while others were in the shape of animals. These mounds were possibly religious ceremonial and burial centers.

About A.D. 800, another culture, the *Mississippian*, developed. The Mississippians lived along the Mississippi River near present-day St. Louis, Missouri. Their capital was called *Cahokia*, and lay at the junction of the Missouri and Mississippi rivers. The Mississippians were also Mound Builders, and they built a large earth mound platform, about 1,000 feet long, and 700 feet wide, in the center of Cahokia. Temples, plazas, and other conical mounds were built around it.

Cahokia was a center for trade along the two rivers. The Mississippians traded food products, leather goods, and pottery with other peoples, both north and south of them. The Mississippian culture was spread throughout the eastern woodlands. The Mississippians were the ancestors of many later Native Americans such as the Creek, Choctaw, Chicksasaw, and many others.

Cahokia had been abandoned by the time the Europeans arrived in the Americas.

The Anasazi

About the same time that the Hopewell culture was developing in the eastern United States, the Anasazi culture was developing in the Southwest. The Anasazi were a highly skilled people who lived and prospered on very dry land in what is today New Mexico, Arizona, Utah, and Colorado. There was little rain, and in order to grow crops, the Anasazi created an irrigation system of canals. These canals ran to the fields. During the rainy season, the streams would overflow into the canals and water the fields.

The Anasazi built large villages of adobe on the sides of cliffs. These villages were like large apartment houses. Many were several stories high and one had more than 800 rooms.

The Anasazi left their villages around 1200 partly because of a long drought. The ruins can still be seen today in the Southwest.

The Anasazi are the ancestors of today's Pueblo, which include the Hopi, Zuni, and Acoma.

Pueblos—large adobe "apartment buildings"—were built on cliffsides by the Pueblo peoples known as the Anasazi.

Europeans Colonize the Americas

Spain, France, and Great Britain all sent explorers to the Americas. Later, they established colonies, which were settled by people seeking freedom, wealth, or adventure. The European governments hoped that the colonies would send them valuable minerals (such as gold and silver), furs, and agricultural products (such as tobacco, lumber, potatoes, indigo, and fur). The colonies provided the European countries with markets for both manufactured goods and slaves.

French explorers claimed the land from Canada through the Great Lakes, and down the Mississippi River to the Gulf of Mexico. They called this territory **New France**. By 1750, almost 100,000 French fur traders and missionaries lived there. Unlike the English, the French did not establish large settlements. Instead, they set up trading posts, and some even lived off the land like the Native Americans. Britain controlled 13 colonies along the Atlantic coast of North America. Spain claimed Florida, establishing a fort at St. Augustine. It also claimed most of what is today Texas, New Mexico, Arizona, and California, as well as present-day Mexico, where it had conquered the Aztec Empire.

By the 1500s, Spain and Portugal had control of Central and South America.

The 13 Original Colonies of the United States of America

New England colonies
Connecticut
Massachusetts
New Hampshire
Rhode Island

Middle colonies
Delaware
Maryland
New Jersey
New York
Pennsylvania

Southern colonies
Georgia
North Carolina
South Carolina
Virginia

Massachusetts, New Hampshire, New York, Rhode Island, Connecticut, New Jersey, Pennsylvania, Delaware, Maryland, Virginia, North Carolina, South Carolina, Georgia

The American Revolution (1775 – 1783)

By 1775, there were serious tensions between the 13 British colonies in North America and the mother country, Great Britain. Among other reasons, the colonists felt they were being taxed too heavily and unfairly because they were not represented in the British Parliament. The British thought it only fair that the colonies should help pay for their defense. Many colonists called for independence from Great Britain. In 1776, the 13 colonies won their revolution against the British, and the United States of America was born.

In 1768, the city of Boston was occupied by British soldiers. These troops were nicknamed *redcoats* because of the color of their jackets. On March 5, 1770, a number of colonists got in an argument with the redcoats and began throwing snowballs and chunks of ice at them. The soldiers fired shots into the angry but unarmed crowd. Five Americans were killed. *Sam Adams* called this event the *Boston Massacre*. The British soldiers were brought to court, Sam Adam's cousin, *John Adams*, defended the soldiers. Two were found guilty of manslaughter and the others were declared innocent. Revolutionaries publicized his story to build support for colonial independence.

Results of the Revolutionary War

1 The 13 colonies became the independent United States of America and were recognized by Great Britain.

2 Britain gave the United States the land east of the Mississippi River, north to Canada, and south to the border of Florida.

3 All British trade restrictions were lifted.

4 A new government with elected representatives was formed under the Articles of Confederation.

5 The successful revolution encouraged other people, especially the French, to overthrow their own governments.

The Liberty Bell, which hangs in Independence Hall in Philadelphia, Pennsylvania, bears an inscription from the Bible: "Proclaim liberty throughout all the land unto all the inhabitants thereof."

4 Mexico

By 1540, within 25 years after **Hernán Cortés** destroyed Tenochtitlán, the capital city of the Aztecs (see p. 58), Spanish explorers claimed land from California to Texas, all along the Gulf coast to Florida, and south to Panama. This entire colony was called **New Spain**.

The people of New Spain were divided into four main groups: Those who had been born in Spain and ruled the colony were called **peninsulares**. The **criollos**, or Creoles, were the children of Spaniards born in New Spain. They often owned large ranches and farms, but were not allowed to hold high government posts. The **mestizos** of Spanish and Indian ancestry, worked as farmers, craftspeople, and laborers. The **native Indians** were forced to work on large farms or in the gold and silver mines.

Mexico was ruled by the Spanish as New Spain for 300 years until the Creoles acted upon their resentment of the peninsulares who ruled Mexico.

Mexican Independence

In 1810, a Creole priest named **Miguel Hidalgo y Costilla**, from the village of Dolores, led a revolt of Mexican Indians and mestizos to Mexico City. Although he was defeated and executed, it was the beginning of the struggle for independence. Ten years later, another revolt, led by **Agustín de Iturbide**, finally broke Spanish rule. Iturbide crowned himself Emperor Agustín I, but his rule did not last. A new congress elected General **Guadalupe Victoria** as the first president of the federal republic in 1824.

After a war with the United States from 1846 to 1848, Mexico lost all of its territory north of the Rio Grande River. In 1862, France took over Mexico. One of Mexico's greatest leaders, a Zapotec Indian named **Benito Juárez**, led the fight to drive out the French. He crushed the regime of the French-installed emperor, the Hapsburg Archduke **Maximilian**, the brother of the Austrian emperor **Franz Josef**. As president of Mexico, Juárez tried to rebuild the country, constructing roads and railroads and supporting free education.

The Mexican Revolution

In 1876, **Porfirio Díaz** took over Mexico, first as president and later as dictator. A mestizo, Díaz ruled for 34 years. He restored order and progress, encouraging foreign investment and industry. Despite this progress, Mexican Indians and other poor people were denied liberty and land.

By 1910, resentment against Díaz was becoming widespread. **Francisco Madero**, a wealthy Creole, wanted to help the poor. He wrote a book about political freedom and traveled around the country telling people about it. When he became popular, Díaz put him in jail. Upon his release, Madero joined forces with **Pancho Villa** (see box), a former bandit, in revolt against Díaz. Díaz fled the country in 1911. **Emiliano Zapata** (see box) led rebels in the south. Zapata's men led raids against the rich and turned over the *haciendas*, or large estates, to the poor.

A new constitution was written in 1917, and the revolution officially ended in the 1920s. In 1934, General **Lázaro Cárdenas** became president. He supported the working class and reformed the land distribution laws, granted freedom of speech, and took over the foreign-owned oil industry.

HEROES OF THE MEXICAN REVOLUTION

Two of the most famous heroes of the Mexican Revolution were Pancho Villa and Emiliano Zapata. Villa led raids in the north, and Zapata in the south.

Pancho Villa had once been an outlaw. He put together an army of bandits and peasants. They robbed the rich, stole cattle, and fought the *federales*, government soldiers. Villa had an unusual hit-and-run style of fighting that made him very popular with the Mexican people. A large man with a roaring laugh, he rode a black horse called Lucifer and twirled his pistols in the air. He always tricked the *federales* and disappeared into the wilderness.

Emiliano Zapata was a rebel leader in the south. He banded together an army of peasants. These workers were loyal to Zapata because he believed the land belonged to them. He rode a great white horse and his battle cry was "land and liberty." He and his men raided large sugar plantations and gave the land back to the peasants who originally farmed it. Zapata's ideas of land reform later became part of the constitution. Both Villa and Zapata were killed and became legends in history and song.

Thousands of women, called *soldaderas*, also joined the revolution. They fought bravely alongside the men. A famous *soldadera* was Adelita. A song was written about her bravery and is still sung today in Mexico.

Pancho Villa

Emiliano Zapata

5 Canada

In 1497, **John Cabot**, a Venetian explorer for England, was the first European since the Vikings to reach Canada. In 1608, a French explorer named **Samuel de Champlain** sailed to Canada and founded the colony of Quebec on the St. Lawrence River. Some years later, in 1670, the English came to Canada and established the **Hudson Bay Company**. This eventually led to a war between England and France.

In 1756, competition for land and the profitable fur trade led to the French and Indian War. England defeated France, which lost nearly all of its holdings in North America. England then took control of Canada.

During the American Revolution, the Canadians remained loyal to England. There were two reasons for this: fear of the power of the United States, and differences in language, culture, and religion. Almost all French Canadians were Roman Catholic and the United States was mostly Protestant.

Canadian Independence

In 1791, the British divided Canada into Upper Canada and Lower Canada. Lower Canada was French-speaking Quebec and Upper Canada was the English-speaking majority. In 1837 the Canadians revolted against the British. The revolt was a failure, however, England recognized that a revolution would happen sooner or later, and allowed the colony to elect its own government. Finally, with the British North America Act of 1867, Canada became the Dominion of Canada. This gave Canada almost full control over its own affairs. It had self-rule, but a governor- general was appointed by the British crown. It was not until 1982 that Canada became totally independent of Britain. At that time, Canadians wrote their own constitution.

The Ten Provinces of Canada

Alberta	**Nova Scotia**
British Columbia	**Ontario**
Manitoba	**Prince Edward Island**
New Brunswick	**Saskatchewan**
Newfoundland	**Quebec**

A maple leaf, the symbol of Canada, appears on the national flag.

Canada also has two territories — The Yukon and the Northwest Territories.
The four original provinces were Ontario, Quebec, Nova Scotia, and New Brunswick.

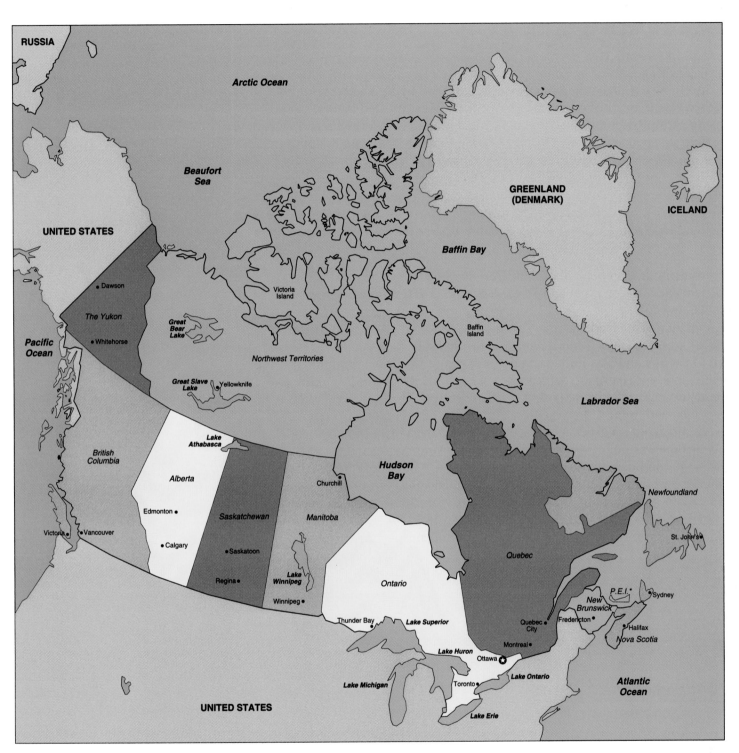

RUSSIA

Arctic Ocean

Beaufort Sea

GREENLAND (DENMARK)

ICELAND

UNITED STATES

Baffin Bay

• Dawson

The Yukon

• Whitehorse

Pacific Ocean

Great Bear Lake

Victoria Island

Baffin Island

Northwest Territories

Labrador Sea

Great Slave Lake • Yellowknife

British Columbia

Lake Athabasca

Alberta

Churchill •

Hudson Bay

Newfoundland

Edmonton •

Saskatchewan

Manitoba

St. John's •

Victoria • • Vancouver

• Calgary

• Saskatoon

Quebec

Regina •

Lake Winnipeg

Ontario

P.E.I. *

• Sydney

New Brunswick

Winnipeg •

Thunder Bay •

Lake Superior

Quebec • City

Fredericton •

• Halifax

Nova Scotia

Montreal •

Lake Huron

Ottawa ✪

Atlantic Ocean

Lake Michigan

Toronto •

Lake Ontario

UNITED STATES

Lake Erie

Canadian Provinces
*The capital of Prince Edward Island is Charlottetown

6 Central and South America

Europeans first arrived in Central and South America in the late 1400s. By the 1500s, nearly all of these lands were controlled by Spain and Portugal. Spurred by the revolutions in other parts of the Western Hemisphere such as the American Revolution in 1776 and Haiti's revolt against the French, which ended in independence for Haiti in 1804, South America began to demand freedom. By the mid-1800s, most countries were independent.

Revolutions

In the early 1800s, a series of rebellions started from Mexico in the north to Argentina in the south. In the south, *José de San Martín* led the fight for independence in Argentina and Peru. *Bernardo O'Higgins* defeated the Spanish in Chile.

In the north, the leader of the fight against Spain was *Simón Bolívar*. Bolívar was a wealthy Venezuelan general. When he was young, he traveled to Europe and was influenced by the ideas of freedom springing up there. Upon his return, he dedicated the rest of his life toward working to liberate Spain's colonies. Starting in 1810, Bolívar fought many battles in Venezuela and in the colony of New Granada, which is today Colombia. One of his major victories was in the Battle of Boyacá in Colombia in 1819. This victory was a turning point in Colombia's struggle for independence.

Bolívar combined his armies with those of San Martín in Peru and Ecuador, captured port cities, and declared the independence of Peru in 1821. However, it was not until 1824 that all of the Spanish were driven out of Peru. Peru and most other countries were free around 1830. A new country was named Bolivia for Bolívar, the great leader of independence.

Simón Bólívar

Brazilian Independence

The Portuguese royal family left Portugal in 1807 when Napoleon threatened their country. They went to Brazil and this became the new center of the Portuguese Empire. King *John IV* ruled until 1821, when he had to return home. His son, *Dom Pedro*, became ruler. The parliament tried to undo King John's reforms and denounced Portugal. Dom Pedro agreed with the Brazilians and refused to return to Portugal. On September 7, 1822, Dom Pedro declared Brazil an independent country. Brazil had won its freedom with very little bloodshed.

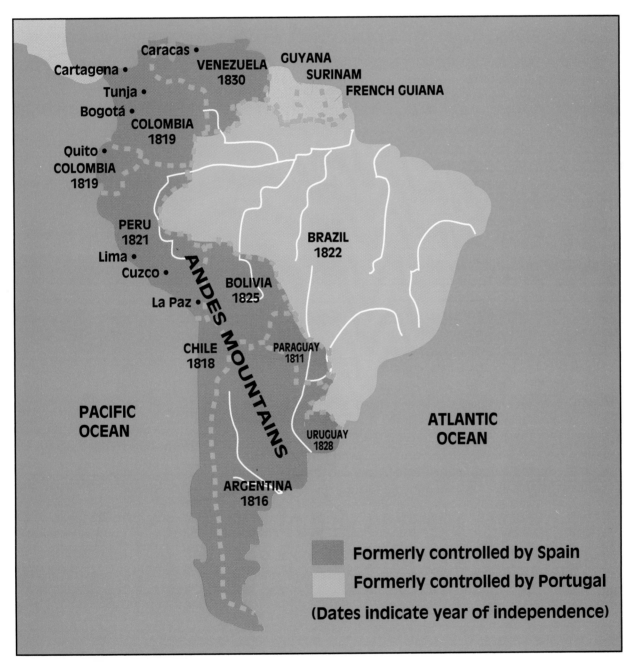

Caracas •
VENEZUELA
1830
Cartagena •
GUYANA
SURINAM
FRENCH GUIANA
Tunja •
Bogotá •
COLOMBIA
1819
Quito •
COLOMBIA
1819
PERU
1821
BRAZIL
1822
Lima •
Cuzco •
ANDES MOUNTAINS
BOLIVIA
1825
La Paz •
CHILE
1818
PARAGUAY
1811
PACIFIC
OCEAN
ATLANTIC
OCEAN
URUGUAY
1828
ARGENTINA
1816

Formerly controlled by Spain
Formerly controlled by Portugal
(Dates indicate year of independence)

South America, about 1822

EUROPE (A.D. 800–1800)

1 The Making of Modern Europe

The era of European history from about A.D. 500 to 1500 is known as the Middle Ages, or the *medieval period*, because the word *medieval* is Latin for "of the middle ages." The era began at the end of the Roman Empire and continued until the modern nations of France and England were established.

Charlemagne's Medieval Empire

Charlemagne was the outstanding ruler in medieval Europe for 46 years, from 768 to 814. A great warrior who extended his kingdom over most of western Europe, by 800, Charlemagne controlled the largest expanse in Europe since the Roman Empire. His aim was not just to rule, but to spread Christianity. *Pope Leo III* was so thankful that he crowned Charlemagne the *Holy Roman Emperor*; his empire would be called the *Holy Roman Empire*.

During his reign, Charlemagne's empire became the most orderly and unified in Europe. He set up a central government and divided his vast holdings into provinces ruled by nobles who reported to him. He built impressive monuments, theaters, and a forum. Charlemagne placed great importance on education and established schools all over his empire.

Holy Roman Empire, about 800

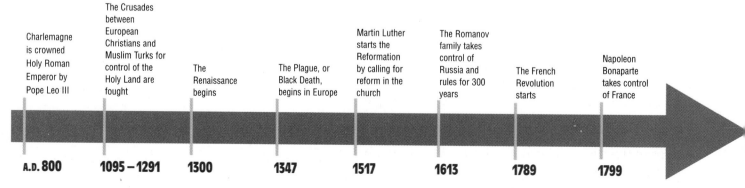

Charlemagne is crowned Holy Roman Emperor by Pope Leo III	The Crusades between European Christians and Muslim Turks for control of the Holy Land are fought	The Renaissance begins	The Plague, or Black Death, begins in Europe	Martin Luther starts the Reformation by calling for reform in the church	The Romanov family takes control of Russia and rules for 300 years	The French Revolution starts	Napoleon Bonaparte takes control of France
A.D. 800	1095 – 1291	1300	1347	1517	1613	1789	1799

William the Conqueror

In 1066, England was invaded by the Normans from France at the the Battle of Hastings. William, duke of Normandy, wanted to defeat the English king **Harold**. After a long battle, Harold was killed and William succeeded him, becoming known as **William the Conqueror**. He was crowned on Christmas Day, 1066. William established a stable government and was responsible for the start of feudalism in England.

The Age of Faith

The Middle Ages is often called the Age of Faith because the church in Rome was more powerful than any government. Most people in Europe were Christians, and religion was the center of life and learning.

Many people dedicated their lives to service in the church. Men became priests and women became nuns. Some became **monks**, religious men who lived in groups outside of society in the countryside or desert. **St. Benedict** of Nursia was one of most well-known monks. He started a **monastery** (a place where monks live), and his order, or group, became known as the Benedictines. The Benedictines built schools, churches, and libraries, and fed the poor. Their organization grew throughout the world by stressing the need to serve others.

Eventually, the Christian church divided. For many years differences had been developing between the eastern and western halves of the church. One of the main differences between the two was over who should head the church. In the East, the Byzantine emperor ruled both church and state. In the West, the pope ruled the church while kings and queens ruled the various countries. Finally, in 1054, the two churches split. The East split off from the church when Pope Leo III crowned Charlemagne Holy Roman Emperor. The eastern division would not recognize this emperor or the pope. In the East, the Christian church became known as the **Eastern Orthodox Church**. In the West, it became known as the **Roman Catholic Church**.

The Feudal System

Feudalism was a system of government and a way of life that restored order in Europe after the fall of Rome. At that time, there were no formal countries but hundreds of kingdoms, or **fiefdoms**. People who were given land were expected to be loyal to the landowner. In return, they were protected against invaders. There were three classes of people during that time. The **nobles** were the kings and lords; priests, bishops, and cardinals were called the **clergy**; and the **peasants** worked as farmers, builders, and craftspeople.

Under the feudal system, nobles (also called lords) gave land and protection to **vassals**, or lesser lords, who usually paid taxes to the lord and provided him with military service. The land the vassal received was called a **manor**. Many of the peasants who worked on the manors were **serfs**. Serfs were not slaves but could not leave the manor unless the lord permitted it. Most of the work done on a noble's large estate was done by serfs.

The lords and ladies lived in castles on the estates. Young nobles in training were called **squires**. Once a squire had learned the skills and duties of a nobleman, he became a soldier for the lord. These soldiers were called **knights**.

The Crusades

The Crusades were a series of religious wars that took place from 1095 to 1291. The purpose of the Crusades was for the European Christians to defeat the Muslim Turks for control of the Holy Land—that part of the Middle East where Jesus had lived, especially the city of Jerusalem. It had been taken by the Seljuk Turks in 1085. When the Seljuks next planned to invade Constantinople, the Byzantines asked for help. *Pope Urban II* organized the Crusades to recapture the Holy Land, but, even after almost 200 years and several major Crusades, the Christians still did not succeed.

Significant Early Crusades

1 **The First Crusade** (1095–1099). **It took the first army of European knights two years to reach Turkey, where they defeated the Turkish army, despite being outnumbered. Later, the knights captured Jerusalem. The Crusaders set up small kingdoms around the cities of Jerusalem, Edessa, Antioch, and Tripoli.**

2 **The Second Crusade** (1147–1149). **The Seljuk Turks recaptured the city of Edessa in 1144. This started a new Crusade that was joined by King Louis VII and his wife, Queen Eleanor of Aquitaine of France (see box).**

3 **The Third Crusade** (1189–1192). **The Third Crusade was caused by the capture of Jerusalem by the Muslim leader Saladin in 1187. This Crusade was led by three kings Frederick I of Germany, Philip II of France, and Richard I of England (Richard the Lion-Hearted). The Third Crusade ended when Richard and Saladin agreed to make peace for five years.**

Crusaders were the knights of Europe. They dressed in the armor and chain mail typical of medieval European times.

Eleanor of Aquitaine and Richard the Lion-Hearted

Eleanor of Aquitaine was one of the first women to challenge the church and her two husbands for equality. Eleanor was born wealthy and had a good education. Her father, *Duke William of Aquitaine*, raised her to rule his land in central and southwestern France. When he died, many men wanted to marry her for control of the land. She married *Louis VII* of France and became queen of France. But Louis would not allow her to rule equally with him despite the fact that she had brought more territory to the kingdom than he had, so Eleanor had the church dissolve her marriage. She then married King *Henry II* of England and had five sons and three daughters, but Henry would not share power with her either.

    Richard I (the Lion-Hearted) was the favorite son of Eleanor. He and two of his brothers had plotted to overthrow their father, Henry II, in 1173. The plan failed, and their father forgave them, so that in 1189, Richard became king of England. He was very popular, but spent much of his ten-year reign fighting in the Crusades. He received the name Richard the Lion-Hearted because he was such a brave and able knight. Legend has it that Richard was so well liked that even his enemy, *Saladin* of Constantinople, said that if he were to lose Jerusalem, he would rather lose it to Richard than to anyone else. During Richard's time away at the Crusades, Eleanor ruled in his place. She governed well, was just, and established some rights for women.

The Magna Carta

King *John* was crowned king of England in 1199 after the death of Richard I. After increasing taxes and having a long feud with the pope, nobles and clergy forced King John to sign the *Magna Carta*, which means "great charter." The Magna Carta strongly limited the power of the king.

MAJOR POINTS OF THE MAGNA CARTA

*   **The king is the absolute ruler but he has to obey the laws.**
*   **The king cannot limit the freedom of the church.**
*   **The king cannot tax land without a meeting of the Great Council, the leading 25 landowners.**
*   **The king cannot put any free person in jail without a trial.**

The Hundred Years' War (1337 – 1453)

The Norman kings of England were the feudal lords over large sections of French territory. The French rulers wanted to reign over their land. The French became angry when King *Edward III* of England claimed to also be king of France. The French invaded English territory and an on-again, off-again war began between England and France; it lasted for over a hundred years. This struggle became known as the Hundred Years' War.

The Hundred Years' War did not end until 1453, when the French drove the English from the city of Bordeaux, France. England would no longer be a power on the continent of Europe.

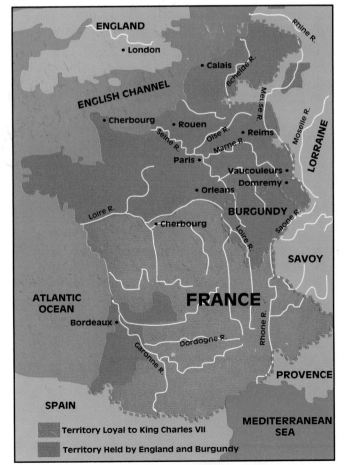

France, about 1400

Joan of Arc

A young girl named *Joan of Arc*, from the French region of Lorraine, led several major battles during the Hundred Years' War. She was only 16 when she convinced Prince Charles of France, later King *Charles VII*, to let her build an army. Joan's clear, direct leadership inspired enthusiasm and resulted in many victories, including the important *Battle of Orléans*. Joan became a heroine, but she was later captured by the English, sentenced to death by a church court for witchcraft and heresy, and burned at the stake. Centuries later, the Catholic church named her a saint.

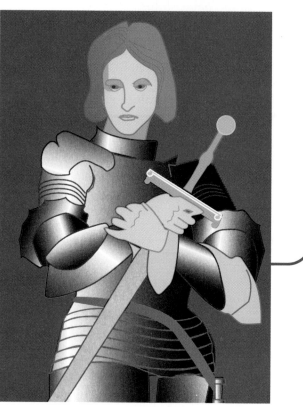

Joan of Arc

The Black Death

In 1347, an Italian ship returned from the east to Messina, Italy. Sailors came ashore bringing with them a terrible disease known as the *Plague* or Black Death. It spread quickly across Europe because people knew little about medicine or the need to be clean. Many thought the Plague was caused by God's anger. About one person in every three died from the Plague between 1347 and 1351. In Paris alone, it is estimated that 50,000 people died.

It was hundreds of years before anyone discovered the cause of the Black Death. It was a germ that came from fleas that lived on rats. The rats could have been controlled by cats, but at that time cats had been slaughtered in great numbers because some people believed they were the agents of the devil.

The Renaissance

The Renaissance was a European revival of learning and the arts that began about 1300 in northern Italy. The Renaissance reached its peak in the early 1500s in Rome. It gradually spread throughout northern Europe, where German and Flemish masters created its final works. Wealthy families became *patrons*, or supporters of the arts, paying for works of art, libraries, books, and buildings. The leading Renaissance patrons were the popes in Rome, the *Medici* family in Florence, the *Sforza* family in Milan, and wealthy merchants in Venice.

The Renaissance produced great artists like *Michelangelo* and *Leonardo da Vinci*. It also was a period of scientific progress and exploration of the world beyond Europe.

Differences between the Renaissance and the Age of Faith

1 It celebrated the individual, rather than the group.

2 Interest in the ideas of ancient Greece and Rome returned.

3 People enjoyed worldly pleasure and rejected the simple lifestyle of feudal times.

Highlights of Renaissance Achievements

Art

Michelangelo Buonarroti. An Italian painter, sculptor, poet, and architect, he painted the Sistine Chapel in the Basilica of St. Peter's in the Vatican, carved the sculptures of *David* and the *Pietà* (which is a statue of Mary and Jesus), and designed the dome of St. Peter's.

Leonardo da Vinci. A painter, sculptor, architect, musician, engineer, and scientist, he was considered a genius. Two of his most famous paintings are *Mòna Lisa* and *The Last Supper*, which shows Jesus with his disciples.

Sandro Botticelli. Known for realistic paintings such as *Venus and Mars* and *Birth of Venus*, this artist celebrated the classical culture of Greece and Rome.

Raphael (Raffaello Santi). Painted many religious works such as the *Sistine Madonna* (Mary, the Mother of Jesus) as well as many other paintings in St. Peter's.

Rembrandt van Rijn. Often considered the greatest painter of northern Europe, he was known for portraits of common people.

Literature

Dante Alighieri. The first to write an important book in Italian, his *Divine Comedy*, a long poem, is considered a literary masterpiece.

Geoffrey Chaucer. The author of *Canterbury Tales*, a collection of stories about traveling pilgrims on their way to the religious shrine in Canterbury, England.

Niccoló Machiavelli. An Italian who wrote a book called *The Prince*, which was a guide book for political rulers on how to gain and maintain power.

Miguel de Cervantes. A Spanish writer whose masterpiece, *Don Quixote*, poked fun at knighthood and feudal society.

William Shakespeare. Considered the greatest English poet and playwright, he wrote many plays, such as *Romeo and Juliet, Julius Caesar,* and *Macbeth*.

Johannes Gutenberg. Inventor of the printing press, about 1455, making it possible to print books cheaply and quickly. Prior to this, books were copied by hand.

Science and Technology

Nicolaus Copernicus. An astronomer who observed that the sun, not Earth, is the center of the universe, contrary to what the church taught people to believe.

Galileo Galilei. An astronomer who improved the telescope and confirmed Copernicus's theory that the planets revolve around the sun.

René Descartes. A mathematician, was the founder of modern geometry.

William Harvey. A doctor who demonstrated that blood circulates throughout the body.

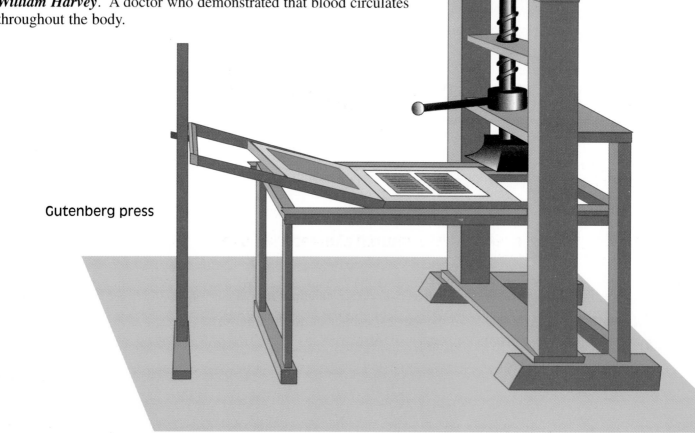

Gutenberg press

The Reformation

The Protestant Reformation was a religious revolt, or protest, against the Roman Catholic Church. A German clergyman, **Martin Luther**, was the person responsible for starting the movement in 1517.

The church had grown very rich and powerful and nearly all Europeans were Catholic. However, some people questioned the church's authority when it began the practice of selling **indulgences**, or pardons, for sin. Believing you shouldn't have to buy your way into heaven, Martin Luther became angry. Luther believed that to gain heaven all you needed was to have faith in God as told in the New Testament. The problem was that most people couldn't read the Bible because it was written in Latin. Luther listed this complaint and others on a statement called the **Ninety-five Theses**. He nailed this statement to the door of the church in Wittenberg, Germany. His writings were printed and distributed and his teachings began to spread over Europe.

In 1521, Pope **Leo X** excommunicated (banned) Luther from the Catholic church, and Holy Roman Emperor **Charles V** declared him an outlaw. While in hiding, he translated the Bible into German so people could read and understand it. Eventually, people left the Catholic church to form their own churches. People who believed Luther's teachings were called **Lutherans**.

Other Protestant movements began all over Europe. In Switzerland, **John Calvin** believed that God had already chosen a group, the elect, for heaven. This group became known as **Calvinists**, and eventually Presbyterians. In England, King **Henry VIII** wanted to divorce his wife, **Catherine of Aragon**. The pope would not grant the divorce. Henry declared that he, not the pope, would be head of the Church of England. Henry and all of England left the Roman Catholic Church. Although the church in England changed little, the pope was no longer its authority.

Martin Luther

Causes of the Reformation

1 The church had become too rich, powerful, and corrupt. People had begun to challenge its authority.

2 Throughout western Europe, everyone had to pay taxes to the church in Rome, and many wanted to stop.

3 Many people resented that the church claimed rule over civil and state affairs.

4 The invention of the printing press gave more people a chance to read the Bible in Latin and, later, in their own languages. With more individuals reading and learning from books, more individuals formed their own ideas.

Catholic Reformation or Counter-Reformation

To defend itself against the Protestant movement, the Catholic church took a number of actions. These actions were called the *Catholic Reformation* or *Counter-Reformation*. These were some of the actions:

Important Events of the Catholic Reformation

1 The church set up courts called the Inquisition. These courts tried to stop Protestantism by declaring Protestants heretics, or nonbelievers, and bringing them to trial. Many Jewish and Muslim believers were also tried. Those found guilty were tortured or killed.

2 The Council of Trent was set up in 1545 by Pope Paul III for bishops and cardinals to review all the teachings of the Catholic church. The council abolished the selling of indulgences, but reaffirmed the pope to be head of the church with the exclusive right to interpret the Bible. The clergy was made to reform.

3 The Society of Jesus was founded by Ignatius of Loyola. Its priests were called Jesuits. The society was set up like an army, to demand complete obedience. The Jesuits were very successful in stopping converts to Protestanism as they became great teachers, opened hospitals, and worked with the poor.

4 The church published a list of books called the Index. These were the books good Catholics were not supposed to read.

European Expansion Overseas

The late 1400s and early 1500s began an age of exploration for European countries. They established trade routes with other countries around the African coast and began looking beyond. The Portuguese were the first to establish a good navy and train its sailors. A Portuguese prince, **Henry the Navigator**, studied pooled information of mapmakers and other travelers' information to make better ships, refine maps, and make better instruments. His work sparked the Age of Exploration. Countries sent explorers because they wanted to establish new trade routes and look for gold and gems. Other countries wanted to establish new colonies or to spread Christianity. It was in pursuit of a route to Asia that Christopher Columbus found North America.

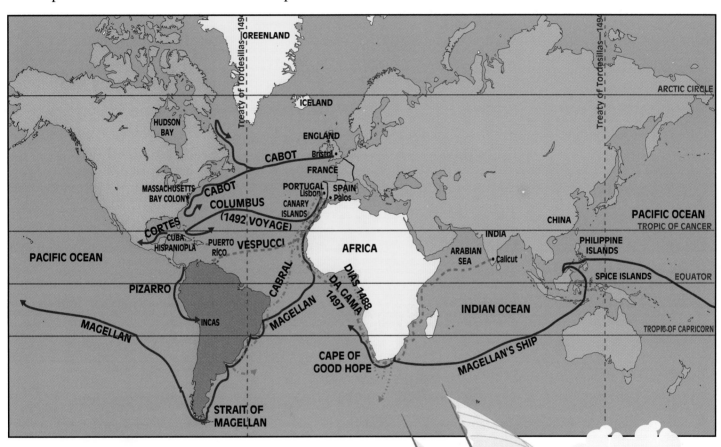

Routes of selected explorers

Early European Explorers (in chronological order)

EXPLORERS	COUNTRY REPRESENTED	YEAR OF EXPLORATION	JOURNEY
Leif Ericson	Vikings (Norway)	1001	Newfoundland
Bartolomeu Dias	Portugal	1487–1488	First European to round Cape of Good Hope at the southern tip of Africa
Christopher Columbus	Spain	1492	San Salvador and West Indies
John Cabot	England	1497	Greenland, Labrador, Newfoundland
Vasco da Gama	Portugal	1497–1498	First to reach India from Europe by sea
Amerigo Vespucci	Spain	1497–1502	South America and West Indies
Pedro Cabral	Portugal	1500	Sailed around Africa to India; Brazil
Vasco de Balboa	Spain	1513	Pacific Ocean
Juan Ponce de León	Spain	1513	Florida
Ferdinand Magellan	Spain	1509–1522	First to sail around the globe
Hernán Cortés	Spain	1519–1521	Aztec kingdom of Mexico
Giovanni da Verrazano	France	1524	Eastern coast of North America
Pánfilo de Narváez	Spain	1528	Florida and Mexico
Francisco Pizarro	Spain	1531	Inca empire of Peru
Jacques Cartier	France	1535	St. Lawrence River
Esteban and Father Marcos	Spain	1539	Canada and Quebec; Zuni pueblos of New Mexico
Hernando de Soto	Spain	1539–1542	Mississippi River, American Southeast
Juan Rodríguez Cabrillo	Spain	1542	California
Francisco de Coronado	Spain	1540–1542	American Southwest
Henry Hudson	Holland	1609	Hudson River and Hudson Bay
Sir Francis Drake	England	1577–1580	Around the world
Samuel de Champlain	France	1603	The Great Lakes and Quebec

The Rise of Absolute Monarchy

During the Middle Ages, kings and queens had limited power because of the feudal lords and the church. Near the end of the Middle Ages, around 1500, the monarchs in many European countries began to expand their power. By the 1600s, some had become *absolute monarchs*, rulers with unlimited power. Their supreme power was acknowledged by lords and commoners, and the church had little power over them.

Absolute Monarchs of Europe

England	
Henry VII (1485 – 1509)	Responsible for establishing the king's authority over nobles.
Henry VIII (1509 – 1547)	Named himself head of the Church of England (see p. 79).
Elizabeth I (1558 – 1603)	Preserved Protestantism in England and achieved world power defeating the Spanish Armada.

France	
Louis XIII (1610 – 1643)	Presided over the French government with Cardinal Richelieu, attaining world power for France.
Louis XIV (1643 – 1715)	Known as the Grand Monarch and the Sun King, he represented the height of absolutism, maintaining an extravagant court at Versailles.

Spain	
Ferdinand and Isabella (1479 – 1516)	Increased royal power over the nobles and became a world power by sending explorers to conquer new lands.
Charles V (1519 – 1556)	Controlled Spain, the Netherlands, southern Italy, Austria, and much of central Europe as Holy Roman Emperor.
Philip II (1556 – 1598)	Controlled the largest empire of the time, but it declined during his reign.

Russia	
Peter the Great (1682 – 1725)	Strengthened his power by creating a strong army and crushing a revolt of the nobles. His government took control of the Russian Orthodox Church.
Catherine the Great (1762 – 1796)	Maintained absolute control and expanded territory.

Prussia	
Frederick the Great (1740 – 1786)	Exerted control as a powerful ruler and general who started the Seven Years' War and added Poland to his realm.

Austria	
Maria Theresa (1740 – 1780)	Successfully fought off numerous attacks for her throne, ruling for 40 years.
Joseph II (1780 – 1790)	Put the Catholic Church under state control and weakened nobles by taxation.

The Enlightenment

The European *Age of Enlightenment* in the early 1700s brought together the ideas of the Renaissance and the *Scientific Revolution*. A group of philosophers tried to bring scientific reasoning to all parts of life. They believed that there were natural laws which, if followed, would make people happy. They were the first Europeans since ancient times to believe that free people could build a better society.

The ideas of the Enlightenment were at the root of both the French and American revolutions. Enlightenment philosophers looked to the writings of the English philosopher *John Locke*, who opposed absolute monarchs. Locke wrote that people have a right to life, liberty, and property. He believed that people made a contract with their government to protect their natural rights.

Enlightenment philosophers in France included Voltaire, Diderot, Montesquieu, and Rousseau. The Scottish economist Adam Smith, the English geographer Captain James Cook, and Americans such as Benjamin Franklin and Thomas Jefferson were all supporters of Enlightenment ideas as well.

The French Revolution (1789)

In 1789, there were three classes of people in France — the clergy, the nobles, and the common people. They were often referred to as the *First Estate* (church), the *Second Estate* (nobles), and the *Third Estate* (common people).

There were great differences in the way the estates lived. The king had total authority. The king and the nobles lived very well and paid few taxes, while the poor struggled and paid most of the taxes. When taxes were raised, the poor often starved.

Fighting wars was expensive, and France went into debt. King *Louis XVI* called a meeting of representatives from each of the three estates to discuss raising money and new taxes. The Third Estate, the common people, tried to use this meeting to reform the government. When the king refused to give them any power, they formed the National Assembly. They met at a tennis court and agreed that they would demand a new constitution and stay together until one was written. This is known as the *Oath of the Tennis Court*.

On July 14, 1789, citizens took over the Bastille, a storehouse of ammunition and the royal prison. This sparked the beginning of the revolution.

The National Assembly put forth the *Declaration of the Rights of Man*. It was written by the *Marquis de Lafayette*, who had helped the Americans with their revolution. The National Assembly declared France a constitutional monarchy. This meant that France would be ruled by a constitution and the power of the monarch would be limited.

The revolution went on for some years and became more violent. The king and queen were tried for treason and publicly executed at the guillotine. France became a republic, but many things did not improve. The summer of 1793 through the summer of 1794 was called the *Reign of Terror* because many of the new leaders had begun to use fear and violence, executing hundreds of people each week. Only after the Reign of Terror and the death of the most ruthless leaders did the revolution end.

The guillotine was widely used during the French Revolution to behead aristocrats of the French monarchy. The device consists of a heavy blade that is dropped between two guideposts onto the neck of those sentenced to death.

Causes of the French Revolution

1 The absolute control of the king and his court was an unfair system of government, a government that was also bankrupt.

2 The rich people of the First and Second estates paid few taxes, while the Third Estate, the common people, paid most of the taxes.

3 The extravagance of the rich and the misery of the poor were extreme. When the king needed even more taxes, the commoners refused.

4 Due in part to France's feudal arrangements, food was scarce. Bread, which was the main part of the peasants' diet, was very high priced by the summer of 1789.

5 The National Assembly was formed to break from the king and form a new government based on a constitution.

The Age of Napoleon (1799 – 1815)

Napoleon Bonaparte was a military genius and leader who created a French empire after the chaos of the revolution. He won so many battles that he became very popular with the people of France. In 1799, at the age of 30, Napoleon overthrew the French government. He prepared a new constitution and became First Consul. He eventually ruled as a military dictator.

Napoleon restored order to France. He brought religious peace because the church accepted him. He changed the tax system and instituted new laws, called the *Napoleonic Code*. This code made laws the same all over France and put an end to the special treatment of nobles. Napoleon then began a series of wars in order to gain new lands.

In 1804, Napoleon changed the republic into an empire and crowned himself Emperor *Napoleon I*. At the height of his power, from 1810 to 1812, France controlled much of Europe, either directly or through the appointments of relatives. Four European countries joined forces in order to stop him, succeeding in 1815 at the *Battle of Waterloo* in Belgium. Napoleon was exiled to the small island of St. Helena until his death.

2 Russia

The Early History

In the 800s, Vikings landed in Russia and set up trade routes on the Russian rivers that led from the Baltic Sea to Constantinople, the capital of the Byzantine Empire. They ruled from two major cities—Kiev and Novgorod. Their ruler was known as the Great Prince of Kiev. Another prince, *Vladimir I*, brought Christianity to Russia. This era of Russian history is known as the *Kievan Period*.

During the European Middle Ages, Russia was invaded by the Tartars, a Mongol people from Central Asia. By 1240, Russia was part of the vast Mongol Empire. The Mongols moved the capital to Moscow, a city in the state of Muscovy. Great Princes of Muscovy ruled the empire. In 1462, *Ivan III* became Great Prince, but he broke from the Mongols in 1480. He declared himself *czar*, which is the Slavic form of "Caesar." Ivan III became known as *Ivan the Great* because he expanded Russia and created religious and political order. He set up a type of feudalism that lasted for hundreds of years. Land was granted to nobles called *boyars*; in return, these boyars gave Ivan military service. Most Russians were peasants who farmed the land. Ivan was also responsible for building great structures, including the *Kremlin*, a group of six magnificent churches in Moscow.

Ivan's grandson, *Ivan IV*, had great victories over the Mongols early in his reign. He expanded Russia and was a just ruler. When his wife, Anastasia, died, he blamed the boyars and probably went insane. He became known as *Ivan the Terrible* because of the many common people he had killed. He even killed his own oldest son. Ivan died in 1584, and a number of civil wars followed.

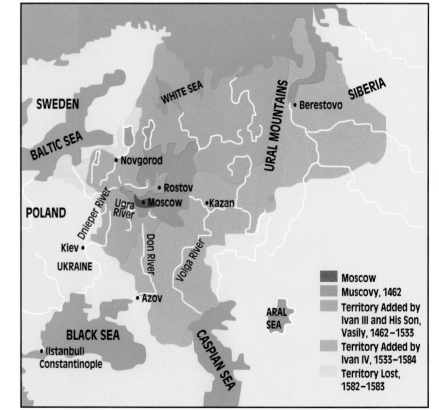

Russian-ruled territories

Russia Becomes a World Leader

The *Romanov* family took control of Russia in 1613 and remained in power for 300 years. In 1682, *Peter Romanov* became czar of Russia and ruled until 1725. His main goal was to modernize Russia, so he traveled to Europe to learn from Europeans. Upon his return, he built factories and schools, modernized the government, and improved the army. He built a new capital, St. Petersburg, and had it designed in the grand style of Europe. Peter, who is called *Peter the Great*, then set out to enlarge the empire and make Russia a major European power. He did so by defeating the Swedes and extending Russia's territory along the Baltic Sea.

Catherine II became empress of Russia in 1762, after her husband, *Peter III*, was removed from the throne. Like Peter the Great, she admired the culture of the West and encouraged writing, art, and music throughout Russia. She also established the first school for girls and was the first to appoint women to important posts. Catherine expanded the empire greatly, taking Poland and all of Turkey and eventually moving eastward to the Pacific Ocean. By the end of her reign in 1796, Russia had become a world power, and she was remembered as *Catherine the Great.*

Onion-shaped domes and colorful decorations are typical of Russian Orthodox churches.

THE MODERN WORLD (1700–PRESENT)

1 After the Renaissance

In the late eighteenth century, the growth of industry and factories made a big change in the way people lived in Europe. By the early twentieth century, more people worked in business and industry than in farming. New technology and inventions made war more terrible than ever before imagined.

The Industrial Revolution

The Industrial Revolution was the time of change when power-driven machinery replaced hand labor. It began in England in the 1760s and later spread to western Europe and the United States. During the next century, many changes were made in how things were produced. Goods began to be made in factories and a number of inventions made production faster. The steam engine, which replaced waterwheels for weaving and spinning mills, was one of the most important inventions. It enabled textile workers to make up to 50 times more cloth than was possible by hand. The textile industry was among the first to be mechanically improved. Also changed were the coal, iron, and steel industries.

The Industrial Revolution also changed the way people lived as they moved from the countryside to the city for factory jobs. The bad effects were that this created overcrowded, often unsanitary housing and miserable factory conditions. The good effects were that more new products were available for more people to own to make their lives easier. Also, the middle class grew and gained more power.

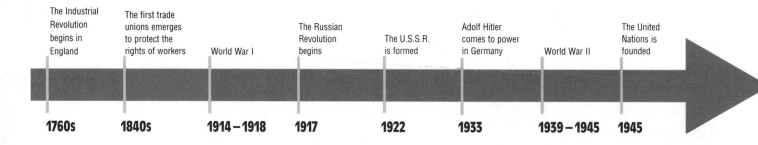

The Industrial Revolution begins in England	The first trade unions emerges to protect the rights of workers	World War I	The Russian Revolution begins	The U.S.S.R. is formed	Adolf Hitler comes to power in Germany	World War II	The United Nations is founded
1760s	1840s	1914–1918	1917	1922	1933	1939–1945	1945

The Rise of Unions

Factory work was brutal. Workers had to labor up to fifteen hours a day in unsafe conditions for very low pay. Children often worked ten hours a day. By the 1840s, efforts were being made to organize workers into trade unions to improve working conditions and increase pay. A ***trade union*** is a group of workers who join together to meet and negotiate with managers or owners for the benefit of workers. The purpose of a trade union is to give workers more power in the belief that groups of workers acting together have greater ability to win their demands than an individual acting alone. As a result of the unions' successes, a number of laws governing the treatment of laborers were passed.

The first laws passed (in Great Britain) as a result of unions:

Factory Act of 1833	Limited children under thirteen to work eight hours a day, six days a week.
Mines Act of 1842	Prohibited employment of children under ten and women from working in mines.
Ten-Hour Law of 1847	Reduced working hours to ten hours a day.

Inventions That Spurred the Industrial Revolution

INVENTOR	INVENTION
James Hargreaves (English)	Spinning jenny (1764). Spins a number of threads at one time.
James Watt (Scottish)	Improvement of the steam engine (1765), which advanced the Industrial Revolution.
Richard Arkwright (English)	Spinning water frame (1769). Used waterpower for spinning thread.
Samuel Crompton (English)	Spinning mule (1779). Combined spinning jenny and water frame.
Edmund Cartwright (English)	Power loom (1785). Used waterpower for weaving.
Eli Whitney (American)	Cotton gin (1793). Removed seeds from cotton.

Scottish inventor James Watt worked as a mathematical instrument maker at the University of Glasgow when he became interested in improving the steam engine. By 1769, he patented his new steam engine designs and, by the mid-1800s, put his idea into production.

In Watt's reciprocating steam engine, steam pushes a cylinder up and down (reciprocally). The engine worked very efficiently and could be used to run large machines created for a variety of different jobs. These large machines replaced the work of humans to usher in the Industrial Revolution.

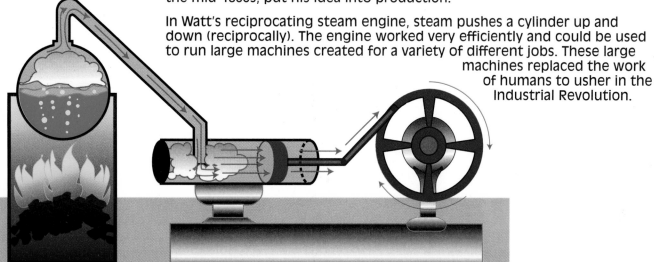

The Rise of Communism

Industrialization brought many social problems. While workers were forced to work long hours for little pay, owners were getting rich. The owners were called *capitalists* because they had the capital — that is, the land, the factories, and the shops.

Some people believed that this new capitalistic system was unfair. They wanted workers, not just owners, to benefit from industrialization. Their ideas became known as *socialism*.

Karl Marx, a German philosopher, and *Friedrich Engels*, an English factory owner, did not believe that the problems of industrialization could be solved within any existing government. They believed a new form of government called *communism* was the answer. Under communism all people would own the factories and farms. The government, as representatives of the people, would own and control all property and businesses. In 1848, they published the *Communist Manifesto*, which outlined their ideas. These ideas spread rapidly, and between 1917 and 1976, more than fifteen countries around the world adopted communism.

Karl Marx

It was Russia that succeeded in the first Communist revolution. Russia had been in a state of unrest for many years. The workers, peasants, and many well-educated people wanted to end the absolute power of the czar and gain a say in the government. By March 1917, half the industrial workers of Petrograd (St. Petersburg) went on strike. People took to the streets and protested food shortages. Soldiers were ordered to stop the revolt, but, instead, they joined in. Czar *Nicholas II* was overthrown.

A Russian named *Lenin* took over the government. His followers were called *Bolsheviks*. Later, they came to be called *Communists*. Civil war broke out in 1918. The czar and 15 million other Russians were killed during the next two years. Lenin and the Bolsheviks formed the Union of Soviet Socialist Republics (U.S.S.R.). It became known as the Soviet Union.

2 World War I (1914-1918)

World War I was the first war in which countries from all over the world took sides. Before it ended, 30 nations on five continents had been involved. When it was over, the map of Europe had changed greatly from the way it looked when the war began. Although it was called "the war to end all wars," the result would lead to another world war among many of the same nations.

World War I was the first modern war in that it was the first time that modern inventions such as airplanes, tanks, submarines, machine guns, and poison gas were widely used. It was also the bloodiest war in history up to that time.

Brief History of World War I

World War I started when Archduke *Francis Ferdinand*, the future ruler of Austria-Hungary, was killed in Sarajevo on June 28, 1914. Austria-Hungary blamed the country of Serbia for his death and declared war on Serbia. This was the first act of World War I.

The countries of Europe had formed alliances with one another. An *alliance* is an agreement among nations to support one another in time of war. Russia, which had promised to support Serbia, prepared its army to fight Austria-Hungary. Germany declared war on Russia and Russia's ally, France. By August 5, all the great powers of Europe were at war. Great Britain, France, and Russia were known as the *Allies*. Germany and Austria-Hungary were called the *Central Powers*. The conflict spread to Japan and Italy on the Allied side and brought the Ottoman Empire (Turkey) among the Central Powers.

Biplanes and tanks were introduced in battle during World War I.

The German army quickly conquered Belgium and moved on to France. At the Battle of Marne, the fighting stopped along an imaginary line called the *Western Front*. It stretched from Belgium on the North Sea, looped through France before heading south, to the border of Switzerland. The war on the Western Front was fought primarily by armies living in trenches that ran along it. Despite heavy fighting over the next four years, neither side gained much territory.

The *Eastern Front* stretched 1,100 miles from the Baltic Sea to the Black Sea. The fighting here was primarily between Russia and Germany and Austria-Hungary. After the Russian government was overthrown, Russia signed a peace treaty with Germany in 1918.

Germany returned to the West. The United States entered the war in 1917 because the Germans had sunk several ships, including the *Lusitania*, a British ship with American passengers. The United States sent nearly two million soldiers to fight. After a number of bloody battles, the Allies finally forced the Germans to retreat and the war ended in November 1918.

ALLIES	CENTRAL POWERS
Great Britain	Germany
France	Austria-Hungary
Russia	Turkey
Italy (from 1915)	Bulgaria
Japan	
United States (from 1917)	

Causes of World War I

Europe before the Treaty of Versailles

1 The industrial countries of Europe were very competitive. Germany and Austria-Hungary, in particular, wanted to increase the size of their empires.

2 Each country began to build up its supply of weapons. Germany increased the size of its navy to compete with England.

3 To protect themselves from empires, countries formed alliances. These agreements stated that if one nation were attacked, the other nations would defend it. France, Russia, and Great Britain had an alliance called the Triple Entente. Germany, Austria-Hungary, and Italy signed the Triple Alliance.

4 In response to the assassination of the Austrian Archduke Ferdinand in Sarajevo, Bosnia, in 1914, Austria-Hungary attacked Serbia, a small country in central Europe.

5 The alliances brought many countries into the war: Russia came to the aid of Serbia. Germany then declared war on Russia. France declared war on Germany. Germany attacked Belgium. Great Britain entered the war to help Belgium and France.

6 Slavs, Czechs, and Slovaks wanted freedom from Austria-Hungary and declared war.

Results of World War I

The *Treaty of Versailles*, which ended the war, set forth these conditions:

1 Germany was to give up territory and colonies to France, Great Britain, Belgium, Denmark, and Poland.

2 To prevent Germany from starting another war, the size of its army was reduced. It was forbidden to have submarines and aircraft.

3 Germany accepted responsibility for starting the war and was penalized $33 million in damages to other nations.

4 The League of Nations was formed (see p. 95).

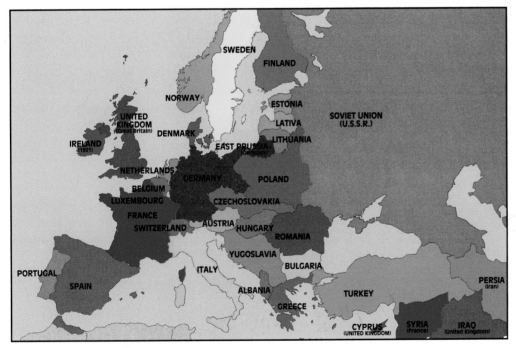

Europe after the Treaty of Versailles

WORLD LEADERS IN WORLD WAR I

Georges Clemenceau. Premier of France and Minister of War during World War I. Clemenceau was nicknamed the Tiger because of his aggressive style. He was 77 years old when the war ended.

David Lloyd George. Prime Minister of Great Britain from 1916 to 1922. Lloyd George wanted to make sure that Germany lost its navy and its empire in World War I. In the treaty that ended the war, he served as the mediator between Clemenceau, who pressed for harsh terms, and U.S. President Woodrow Wilson, who tended to be more generous.

Czar Nicholas II. Nicholas II was the last czar (king) of Russia. He was forced from the throne in 1917 when the war was not going well for Russia. He and his family were murdered in 1918 by the Bolsheviks, a revolutionary party.

Kaiser Wilhelm II. A grandson of Queen Victoria of England, Wilhelm ruled Germany from 1888 to 1918. He fled to Holland to avoid capture after Germany was defeated.

Woodrow Wilson. The twenty-eighth President of the United States, Wilson did his best to keep the United States out of the war. After the war was over, he promoted the ***League of Nations*** (see p. 95) to help solve disputes peacefully between countries.

Georges Clemenceau   Kaiser Wilhelm II   Czar Nicholas II

₃ The League of Nations

U.S. President Woodrow Wilson proposed the League of Nations to prevent war by settling disputes between nations through peaceful talks. It was established in January 1920 after World War I, but the United States never joined, and the league fell apart at the start of World War II, in 1939. It was officially dissolved in April 1946, when the *United Nations* began operations.

Woodrow Wilson

The League of Nations Fails

In its early years, the League of Nations settled some disputes between nations. In some cases, it even prevented war. But still it failed, mostly because of these problems:

1 The league did not include every major nation. The United States never joined. Russia joined in 1934, but was later removed. Germany and Japan withdrew in 1933.

2 Decisions required that all countries agree, a rare occurrence.

3 The league had no power to tax its members, and had to rely on voluntary contributions of its members.

4 It could not raise an army to enforce its decisions.

5 It was unable to prevent Japan from invading Manchuria (on the Asian mainland), or Italy from conquering Ethiopia (in Africa), or the Chaco War between Bolivia and Paraguay.

４ World War II (1939-1945)

Brief History of World War II

Adolf Hitler came to power in Germany in 1933. He was a ruthless dictator who wanted to control Europe and eventually the world. In March 1938, Germany annexed Austria and took it over. Great Britain, France, and the Soviet Union protested, but did nothing.

Hitler next announced he would take Sudetenland, a part of Czechoslovakia, by force if necessary. Czechoslovakia had an alliance with Great Britain and France that obliged them to defend Czechoslovakia if attacked. Britain and France wanted to avoid a war and gave the Sudetenland to Hitler assuming he would now stop. Six months later, Hitler broke his promise and took over the rest of Czechoslovakia as well. In 1939, German troops took over Poland. Britain and France declared war.

Germany then conquered Denmark, Norway, the Netherlands, Belgium, and Luxembourg, and forced France to surrender. By 1940, Hitler controlled much of Western Europe. Germany then turned on Britain by bombing its cities. When this failed, it attacked the Soviet Union, which then joined the Allies.

The United States entered the war on the side of the allies on December 8, 1941, the day after Japan bombed Pearl Harbor in Hawaii. By the end of the year, the United States was also at war with Germany and Italy.

After two years of war, Soviet troops defeated 200,000 Germans at Stalingrad in 1943. They pushed the German troops out of the Soviet Union and then attacked Germany.

In Western Europe, the Allies defeated Italy and were planning a massive invasion to liberate France. This secret invasion was known as D day. On June 6, 1944, the Allies, led by General *Dwight D. Eisenhower* of the United States, landed and soon freed France and Belgium. Then the Allies invaded Germany. On May 8, 1945, Germany surrendered.

The Pacific War

The war in the Pacific between the United States and Japan continued until August 1945. The Japanese had seized Hong Kong and Singapore, and invaded the Philippines. Earlier, Japan had also seized Korea, Manchuria, and parts of China. In Southeast Asia, Japanese armies took Thailand, Burma, and the Dutch West Indies. Not until June 1942, was the United States able to stop them with the *Battle of Midway Island*. This was the turning point of the war in the Pacific and forced the Japanese to retreat. The Japanese were losing the war, but would not surrender. In August 1945, the United States dropped *atomic bombs* on the Japanese cities of *Hiroshima* and *Nagasaki*. Japan surrendered.

By the end of the war, the total world deaths were 30 to 40 million, but it is impossible to guess the number of persons who were wounded or disabled. There were millions of soldiers from 40 countries involved in World War II, and it was fought on six continents.

ALLIES	AXIS
Great Britain	Germany
France	Soviet Union (until 1941)
Canada	Japan
United States (from 1941)	Italy
Soviet Union (from 1941)	
China	

Causes of World War II

1 The failure of the Treaty of Versailles (see p. 93) to bring lasting peace after World War I. Many Germans found the settlement insulting, thinking it punished their country unfairly.

2 Dictators in Germany, Japan, and Italy promoted a fanatical national pride, called fascism. They believed this pride was stronger than that in democratic nations where government ruled with the consent of the people.

3 The Axis powers (Germany, Japan, and Italy) wanted to conquer their neighbors. Japan wanted to create a New Order in Asia; Italy wanted to rule much of Africa; and Germany wanted to rule Europe and eventually the world. Each invaded other countries and replaced their governments with military dictatorships.

4 A terrible worldwide economic depression hit Germany especially hard because of the war reparations it had been forced to make.

Dictatorships

A *dictator* is a ruler who has absolute power. A *dictatorship* is a type of government with total control over its people. The ambitions of dictators like Hitler, Mussolini, and Stalin helped steer the world into World War II.

Nazi Germany and Adolf Hitler

Adolf Hitler was originally an artist from Austria. He became involved in politics and joined the National Socialist German Workers' Party, also known as the *Nazis*. Hitler was a good organizer and speaker. He rose to power by combining terror with skillful *propaganda* (information spread to promote a cause or idea). His promise of jobs and to restore German greatness won him a large following. He became chancellor of Germany in 1933, turning the country into a brutal and terrifying dictatorship. Immediately, he started a new empire called the *Third Reich*, and took the title *führer*, which means "leader." He banned all political parties except the Nazi party, burned all books not liked by the Nazis, and cracked down on all religions that did not agree with him.

The Nazi movement was based on extreme love of country, German greatness, and hate. Hitler preached hatred of Jews, and thought everyone but Germans were inferior, or not even human. These beliefs led him to kill Jews and conquer other countries to expand Germany (see Holocaust, p. 99).

Stalin's Soviet Union

Josef Stalin was a revolutionary who became head of the Soviet Union and the Communist Party after Lenin's death. He was a ruthless and ambitious dictator who dealt severely with political opponents. Using the feared secret police, he forced his rivals into exile or had them killed.

Stalin ruled the Soviet Union for 30 years by fear and terror. He also modernized the country, built industry, and increased military power. He collectivized all the farms, taking them from their private owners, often after killing the landowners. He made the Soviet Union a world power again, helped defeat Nazi Germany, and took over most of eastern Europe. He died in 1953.

Fascist Rule of Mussolini in Italy

Benito Mussolini was founder of the Italian *Fascist Party*. He became prime minister in 1922 and turned Italy into a dictatorship. Mussolini wanted to create an Italian empire. He invaded and captured Ethiopia in North Africa in 1935 and Albania in the Balkans in 1939. After forming an alliance with Germany, he became dependent on the Nazis and relied on their support during World War II. When the Allies moved into Italy, Mussolini was captured, but he was rescued by the Germans. Mussolini was captured again in 1945 and killed.

THE HOLOCAUST:
Nazi Germany's War Against the European Jews

In one of the most tragic chapters of World War II, Nazi Germany organized the murder of millions of Jews and other people. This dark period is known as the *Holocaust.* (A holocaust is a disaster that wipes out life.) The Holocaust was not a dispute over land or a power struggle. It was an attempt by the Nazis to rid Germany of "impure" people who did not match their idea of an ideal race.

Adolf Hitler dreamed of a world ruled by blue-eyed, blond, white people he called Aryans. He particularly wanted to rid the world of Jews and built many walled-off prison areas called *concentration camps* in Germany and Poland. Some were work camps, where prisoners made supplies for the German army. Others were death factories, where people were either killed, tortured, or left to die. Hitler sent Jews and anyone who opposed his rule to these concentration camps.

Six million out of 8 million European Jews were killed. Some 5 million other people, including gypsies, the disabled, homosexuals, and political opponents of the Nazis were also killed. Never before had organized murder taken place on such a horrifying scale.

In Nazi concentration camps, prisoners lived in cramped quarters with no personal possessions, except for the clothes on their backs and the dish issued them for food, if food was provided at all.

OTHER LEADERS FROM WORLD WAR II

Neville Chamberlain. Prime Minister of Great Britain at the beginning of World War II, Chamberlain was sure that Hitler could be satisfied, or appeased, by giving him more territory. In 1938, he attended a conference with Hitler, Mussolini, and the French premier where he agreed to give Hitler Sudetenland, part of Czechoslovakia. Chamberlain was replaced by *Sir Winston Churchill.*

Sir Winston Churchill. Elected prime minister of Great Britain in 1940, he was an inspiring speaker, writer, and statesman who favored taking a strong stand against Hitler. His courageous leadership and defiant speeches kept British morale high during Britain's worst days of the war. In 1953, he won the Nobel Prize in literature for his memoirs.

Dwight D. Eisenhower. The supreme commander of the Allied forces, General Eisenhower organized the massive Allied invasion of the French coast on D day in 1944. In 1952, he was elected president of the United States.

Douglas MacArthur. General MacArthur was commander of U.S. force in the Pacific during World War II; later he oversaw the conversion o Japan to a peace-time economy. A man not used to taking orders, MacArthur was later fired by President *Harry S Truman* for not follow ing orders during the Korean War.

Franklin Delano Roosevelt. The only U.S. president to be elected to four terms, Franklin Roosevelt served during two great crises in American history — the Great Depression and World War II. During his entire presidency, Roosevelt was partially paralyzed by polio. He died just three weeks before Germany surrendered.

Hideki Tojo. Head of the military government that ruled Japan after World War I, Tojo was premier from 1941 to 1944. He wanted to build a New Order in Asia with Japan as its leader. At the end of the war, he was executed as a war criminal.

Harry S Truman. Vice President Harry Truman became president when Franklin Roosevelt died. It was his final decision to drop two atomic bombs on Japan, which led to its surrender. After the war, he guaranteed American aid to any country resisting communism.

German fighter planes

Results of World War II

1 Thirty to 40 million people lost their lives.

2 It was the most expensive war in history, costing over $1 trillion and leaving extensive property damage.

3 Millions of people in Europe and Asia lost their homes. Some were unable even to return to their countries. They needed help to start new lives.

4 Japan got a new constitution and a more democratic government.

5 Germany (and its capital, Berlin) was divided and eventually made into two countries. West Germany became an independent democracy. East Germany became a Communist country closely watched by the Soviet Union.

6 The United States and the Soviet Union became the chief world powers, and their differences led to the Cold War (see p. 104), which lasted for the next 40 years.

7 The United Nations was formed (see p. 103 – 104).

Sherman tank

The United Nations

The United Nations (UN) was founded in 1945 to maintain world peace and security. U.S. President Franklin Roosevelt, Winston Churchill of Great Britain, and Josef Stalin of the Soviet Union worked together to form this new organization. The U.S. Congress agreed to allow the United States to join because it came to believe that future wars could be avoided through international cooperation.

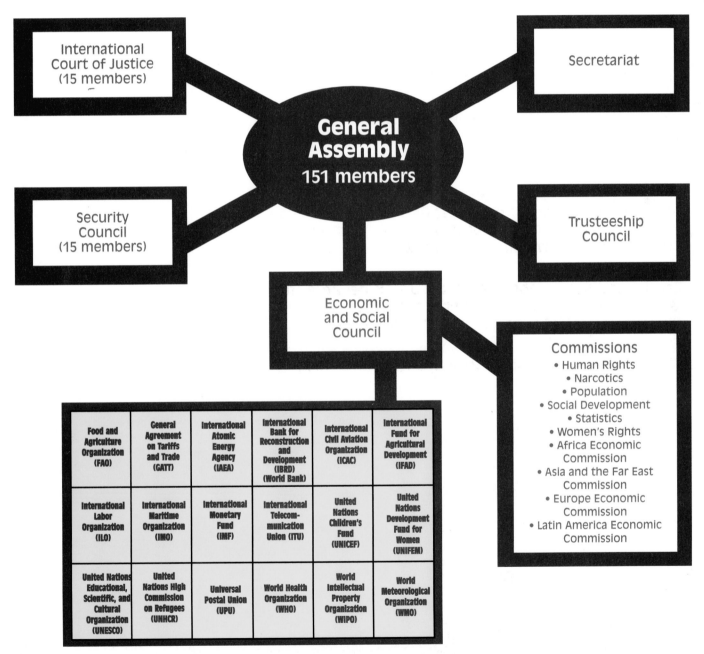

United Nations and its branches

Organization of the United Nations

The *General Assembly* is made up of all members of the UN. Each member has one vote. The General Assembly can make recommendations, but cannot give orders to act.

The *Security Council* is made up of 15 members. There are 5 permanent members—the United States, Great Britain, France, Russia, and China. The other 10 members are elected to two-year terms. Only the Security Council can order the UN to take action. To do this, 9 of the 15 members must vote for action. All 5 permanent members must also vote in favor of the action. Any one of the permanent members can veto or reject an issue. Along with the General Assembly, it meets in New York City.

The *Secretariat* consists of the *Secretary-General* and his or her staff. They are responsible for the daily running of the organization. The Secretary-General is appointed by the General Assembly for a five-year term.

The *International Court of Justice* is made up of 15 judges who decide cases by majority vote. When nations submit their cases to the court, they agree to accept its decision. The court meets in The Hague in the Netherlands.

The Cold War

Following World War II, the Soviets remained in most of the countries they freed, including Poland, Hungary, Czechoslovakia, Bulgaria, and East Germany. The Soviet Union also supported governments in the countries friendly to them. This led to tension between the Soviet Union and the major non-Communist nations, especially the United States. British Prime Minister Winston Churchill declared, "An iron curtain has descended across the continent" (meaning Europe). This *Cold War* lasted from the 1940s to the 1980s, as both the Soviet Union and the United States sought to protect their interests and gain allies around the world. It ended with the destruction of the Berlin Wall in 1989 and the breakup of the Soviet Union in 1991.

6 Events Since World War II

1944 – 1946: The Cold War begins.

1946: The Philippines gain independence from United States; war breaks out in Indochina between colonial France and Vietnamese Communists and Nationalists.

1947 – 1948: Soviet support helps Communist dictatorships seize power across eastern Europe; Pakistan and India gain independence.

1948: The State of Israel is founded; South Africa creates apartheid.

1949: North Atlantic Treaty Organization (NATO), comprised of Western democracies, is formed; the members are the United States, Canada, Iceland, Norway, Britain, the Netherlands, Denmark, Belgium, France, Luxembourg, Portugal, Italy, Greece and Turkey (both joined in 1952), West Germany (joined in 1955), and Spain (joined in 1982); Mao Tse-tung establishes People's Republic of China; Nationalists under Chiang Kai-shek flee to Taiwan; the Soviets build atomic bomb.

1950: The Korean War begins; the Communist army of North Korea invades South Korea; U.S. President Harry S Truman sends troops to South Korea's defense and asks the backing of the United Nations; General Douglas MacArthur leads the UN troops to stop the North Koreans.

1952: Britain's King George VI dies and Queen Elizabeth II is crowned.

1953: Dwight D. Eisenhower is elected president of the United States; the Korean War ends in stalemate; Stalin dies in the Soviet Union.

1954: The French leave Indochina; Vietman divides into the Communist North and non-Communist South.

1955: The Warsaw Pact, comprised of Communist dictatorships, is formed in response to NATO; the members are the Soviet Union, Albania, Bulgaria, Czechoslovakia, East Germany, Hungary, Poland, and Romania; Nikita Khrushchev becomes the Soviet leader.

1956: Hungarians revolt against Communist rule, but are stopped by Soviet troops; Martin Luther King, Jr., rises as leader of the nonviolent civil rights movement in the United States; Egypt nationalizes Suez Canal; with British and French support, Israel recaptures the canal; UN peacekeeping force steps in to give the canal back to Egypt.

1957: The Soviet Union launches the first satellite, *Sputnik*, into space; the modern nation of Ghana wins independence from Great Britain, the first of 38 new countries on the African map by 1968.

1958: The Soviet Union gives loan to Egypt to build the Aswan Dam on the Nile River.

1959: Fidel Castro overthrows the Fulgencio Batista government of Cuba and becomes dictator.

1960: John F. Kennedy is elected president of the United States; Senegal under Leopold Senghor becomes one of Africa's few true democracies.

1961: Communists build the Berlin Wall across the divided city of Berlin in East Germany to prevent citizens from fleeing to the West; U.S. Bay of Pigs invasion fails to free Cuba of the Castro dictatorship.

1962: The Soviet Union puts nuclear missiles in Cuba and triggers fears of nuclear war with the United States; Algeria wins independence from France after a 70-year war.

1963: U.S. President John F. Kennedy is assassinated; Lyndon B. Johnson becomes president.

1964: The U.S. Civil Rights Act makes racial discrimination illegal; China explodes its first atomic bomb.

1965: President Johnson sends U.S. combat troops to Vietnam.

1966: Indira Gandhi becomes Indian prime minister; the Cultural Revolution in China creates chaos.

1967: In retaliation for Egypt's takeover of the Gulf of Aqaba, Israel launches the Six-Day War, in which it is victorious; Israeli troops remain in the Sinai Peninsula, taken from Egypt, the Golan Heights, taken from Syria, and the West Bank, taken from Jordan; Israel takes complete control of Jerusalem.

1968: Martin Luther King, Jr., and Senator Robert Kennedy are assassinated; Richard Nixon is elected president of the United States; Warsaw Pact troops take over Prague, the capital of Czechoslovakia, putting down its reforms of communism; Kenya becomes independent and grows strong under Jomo Kenyatta; fighting breaks out in Northern Ireland between Protestants and Roman Catholics.

1969: U.S. astronauts are the first humans to land on the moon.

1970: Socialist Salvadore Allende is elected president of Chile.

1971: East Pakistan wins independence from Pakistan and becomes the nation of Bangladesh; dictator Idi Amin siezes power in Uganda; 500,000 people die as a result of his brutality and the revenge that follows after he is driven into exile in 1979.

1972 : Ceylon becomes the Republic of Sri Lanka; U.S. president Richard Nixon visits China; Watergate break-in starts the chain of events that lead to the end of the Nixon presidency; Palestine Liberation Organization (PLO) terrorists kill Israeli athletes at Olympics in Munich, Germany; Britain takes control of Northern Ireland after years of violence between Protestants and Catholics; Philippine president Ferdinand Marcos seizes power as dictator.

1973: United States pulls troops out of Vietnam; Arab forces attack Israel on the Jewish holiday of Yom Kippur; after heavy casualties on both sides, an uneasy truce is called; Organization of Petroleum Exporting Countries (OPEC) protests U.S. support for Israel and sharply cuts oil production, triggering a crisis in the United States; General Augusto Pinochet overthrows the Allende government in Chile; Allende dies.

1974: Richard Nixon resigns; Gerald Ford becomes president of the United States.

1976: Jimmy Carter is elected president of the United States; Mao Tse-tung of China dies; the Second Revolution begins to open agriculture and industry to individuals in China.

1977: At Camp David, Maryland, Egypt's Anwar Sadat agrees to recognize Israel's right to exist and Israel's Menachem Begin agrees to return the Sinai Peninsula to Egypt.

1978: Teng Hsiao-p'ing becomes the leader of China.

1979: Margaret Thatcher is named the first female prime minister of England; Iran holds U.S. citizens hostage; the United States establishes diplomatic relations with China; Muslim Fundamentalists take over Iran.

1980: Black majority rule comes to Zimbabwe; Ronald Reagan is elected president of the United States; eight-year war between Iran and Iraq begins.

1981: Anwar Sadat is assassinated by Muslim Fundamentalists in Egypt.

1983: Raul Alfonsin is elected president of Argentina in the first free election there in 40 years.

1984: Indira Gandhi is killed; Rajiv Gandhi, her son, becomes prime minister of India.

1985: Mikhail Gorbachev is named general secretary of the Soviet Union.

1985–1990: Gorbachev institutes policies of *perestroika* (restructuring) and *glasnost* (openness) in the Soviet Union.

1986: President and dictator Ferdinand Marcos flees the Philippines; Corazon Aquino becomes president.

1987: The Iran-Contra hearings explore possible White House crimes in connection with aiding Nicaraguan Contras (counter revolutionaries).

1988: Pakistani president Zia-ul Itaq is killed; Benazir Bhutto becomes prime minister; George Bush is elected president of the United States; Iran-Iraq war ends with Iraq under Saddam Hussein victorious over Muslim Fundamentalists; Palestine Liberation Organization (PLO) recognizes Israel's right to exist.

1989: The Berlin Wall falls, signaling the end of the Cold War.

1989–1990: Communist dictatorships fall throughout eastern Europe now that it is clear Gorbachev will not back them up by military force; war in the Persian Gulf; the United States and international military force fights to keep Iraq out of Kuwait; the Soviet Union dissolves into many separate countries.

1991: A military coup against Gorbachev fails in August, but he is voted out of office and replaced by Boris Yeltsin; civil war breaks out in Yugoslavia.

1992: Bill Clinton is elected president of the United States. Yugoslavia is broken into Bosnia, Croatia, and Slovenia.

1993: Czechoslovakia divides into two countries; the General Agreement on Tariffs and Trade (GATT) makes trade easier between nations while the North American Free Trade Agreement (NAFTA) eases trade barriers between Canada, the United States, and Mexico

1994: Nelson Mandela becomes the first elected black president of South Africa; PLO chairman Yasir Arafat enters Palestinian soil for the first time in 23 years as a result of a new accord with Israel.

APPENDIX: THE WORLD IN FOCUS

Area and Population: The size of a country and the number of its people. Divide population by area to get **population density** (number of people per square mile).

Urban Population: This number is the percentage of a country's total population that lives in urban areas. (Subtract this figure from 100 to get the rural population.)

CUBA	42,400	73	Havana	Spanish
	11,100,000	0.8		

Population Annual Rise: This number shows the percentage of the increase in a nation's population in one year. Countries with high figures may face many problems.

Major Languages Spoken: Noting the languages spoken by a country's people may give you insights into how it was settled and where its people come from.

	AREA (SQ MI) POPULA-TION	URBAN POP. (%) POP. ANNUAL RISE (%)	CAPITAL	MAJOR LANGUAGES	FORM OF GOVERNMENT[1] AND HEAD	DATE OF INDEP.[2] % OF POP. UNDER AGE 15	LITERACY RATE (%)[3] LIFE EXPECT-ANCY	PER-CAPITA GDP[4] HDI
AFGHANISTAN	251,770 17,800,000	18 2.8	Kabul	Pashtu, Tajik, Uzbek, others	Transitional government; President Burhaddin Rabbani	1919 46	44/14 42/43	$200 0.21
ALBANIA	10,580 3,400,000	36 1.8	Tiranë	Albanian, Greek	Democratic multiparty system; President Sali Berisha	1912 33	NA 69/75	$760 0.71
ALGERIA	919,590 27,900,000	50 2.5	Algiers	Arabic, French, Berber dialects	Military-backed government; President Liamine Zeroual	1962 44	70/46 66/68	$1,570 0.55
ANDORRA	175 61,960	65 3.3	Andorra la Vella	Catalan, French, Castilian	Council of 28 members; Executive Council President Oscar Ribas Reig	1278 NA	NA 74/81	$14,000 NA
ANGOLA	481,350	28	Luanda	Portuguese	Emerging multiparty system; President José Eduardo dos Santos	45	44/48	0.27
ANTIGUA AND BARBUDA	170 100,000	31 1.2	St. John's	English, local dialects	Multiparty parliamentary government; Prime Minister Lester Bird	1981 26	NA 71/75	$6,600 0.80
ARGENTINA	1,056,640 33,900,000	86 1.3	Buenos Aires	Spanish, English, Italian, German	Multiparty republic; President Carlos Saúl Menem	1816 30	96/95 68/74	$3,400 0.85
ARMENIA	11,500 3,700,000	68 1.4	Yerevan	Armenian, Russian, others	In transition; President Levon Ter-Petrosyan	1991 31	NA 67/73	NA 0.80
AUSTRALIA	2,941,290 17,800,000	85 0.8	Canberra	English, aboriginal langs.	Multiparty parliamentary government; Prime Minister Paul Keating	1901 22	100/100 74/80	$16,700 0.93
AUSTRIA	31,940 8,000,000	54 0.2	Vienna	German	Multiparty federal republic; Chancellor Franz Vranitzky	1918 18	99 73/79	$18,000 0.92
AZERBAIJAN	33,400 7,400,000	54 1.9	Baku	Azeri, Russian, Armenian, others	In transition; President Heydar Aliyev	1991 33	NA 67/75	NA 0.73
BAHAMAS	3,860 300,000	64 1.5	Nassau	English, some Creole	2-party parliamentary government; Prime Minister Hubert Ingraham	1973 30	90/89 69/76	$10,200 0.85
BAHRAIN	260 600,000	81 2.4	Manama	Arabic, English, Farsi, Urdu	Constitutional monarchy; Amir 'Isa bin Salman Al Khalifa	1971 32	82/69 69/73	$7,800 0.79
BANGLADESH	50,260 116,600,000	14 2.4	Dhaka	Bangla, English	Multiparty parliamentary government; Prime Minister Khaleda Zia	1971 44	47/22 54/53	$200 0.31
BARBADOS	170 300,000	38 0.7	Bridgetown	English	2-party parliamentary government; Prime Minister Lloyd Erskine Sandiford	1966 25	99/99 73/78	$7,000 0.89
BELARUS	80,200 10,300,000	67 0.1	Minsk	Byelorussian, Russian, others	Constitutional democracy; President Aleksandr Lukashenko	1991 23	NA 66/76	NA 0.85
BELGIUM	11,750 10,100,000	97 0.2	Brussels	Flemish, French, German	Multiparty parliamentary constitutional monarchy; Premier Jean-Luc Dehaene	1830 18	99/99 73/80	$17,800 0.92

Fast Facts on 191 Countries

Form of Government and Head: This describes the type of government and gives the title and name of the person who heads it.

Literacy Rate: This is the percentage of people (males/females) who can read and write. A single number is for the percentage for the country as a whole.

Per-Capita GDP: The value of all goods and services produced within a country (its gross domestic product), divided by its population.

-party Communist state; President	1902	95/93	$1,370
del Castro Ruz	23	75/79	0.67

% of Population Under Age 15: Developing countries with a high percentage of young people may have trouble providing a job for everyone who wants one.

Life Expectancy: This is the number of years of life expected at birth. The first number is the life expectancy for males; the second, for females.

HDI (Human Development Index): Use this number—based on life expectancy, adult literacy rate, and purchasing power—to help you compare quality of life.

	AREA (SQ MI) POPULA-TION	URBAN POP. (%) POP. ANNUAL RISE (%)	CAPITAL	MAJOR LANGUAGES	FORM OF GOVERNMENT[1] AND HEAD	DATE OF INDEP.[2] % OF POP. UNDER AGE 15	LITERACY RATE (%)[3] LIFE EXPECT-ANCY	PER-CAPITA GDP[4] HDI
BELIZE	8,800 200,000	48 3.3	Belmopan	English, Spanish, Maya, Garifuna	2-party parliamentary government; Prime Minister Manuel Esquivel	1981 44	91/91 66/70	$1,635 0.67
BENIN	42,710 5,300,000	38 3.1	Porto-Novo	French, Fon, Yoruba, others	Multiparty republic; President Nicephore Soglo	1960 47	32/16 45/48	$410 0.26
BHUTAN	18,150 800,000	13 2.3	Thimphu	Dzongkha, Ne-pali, Tibetan	Constitutional monarchy; King Jigme Singye Wangchuck	1949 39	NA 50/48	$200 0.25
BOLIVIA	418,680 8,200,000	58 2.7	La Paz & Sucre	Spanish, Que-chua, Aymara	Multiparty republic; President Gonzalo Sánchez De Lozada	1825 42	85/71 59/64	$670 0.53
BOSNIA AND HERZEGOVINA	19,740 4,600,000	34 0.7	Sarajevo	Serbo-Croatian	Parliamentary democracy; Presi-dent Alija Izetbegovic	1992 23	95/77 70/75	$3,200 NA
BOTSWANA	218,810 1,400,000	26 2.7	Gaborone	English, Setswana	Multiparty parliamentary republic; President Sir Ketumile Masire	1966 48	32/16 59/65	$2,450 0.67
BRAZIL	3,265,060 155,300,000	76 1.7	Brasília	Portuguese, Spanish, others	Multiparty federal republic; President Itamar Franco	1822 35	82/82 64/71	$2,350 0.76
BRUNEI	2,030 300,000	58 2.6	Bandar Seri Begawan	Malay, English, Chinese	Monarchy; Sultan and Prime Minister Bolkiah Hassanal	1984 36	85/69 69/73	$8,800 0.83
BULGARIA	42,680 8,400,000	67 -0.2	Sofia	Bulgarian, others	Multiparty parliamentary republic; President Zhelyu Mitev Zhelev	1908 20	93 68/75	$3,800 0.82
BURKINA FASO	105,710 10,100,000	21 3.1	Ouagadougou	French, Sudanic languages	Military government; Captain Blaise Compaore	1960 48	28/9 48/49	$350 0.20
BURUNDI	9,900 6,000,000	6 2.9	Bujumbura	Kirundi, French, Swahili	Multiparty republic; President Melchior Ndadaye	1962 46	61/40 46/50	$205 0.28
CAMBODIA	68,150 10,300,000	13 2.9	Phnom Penh	Khmer, French	Constitutional monarchy; Prime Ministers Norodom Ranariddh & Hun Sen	1949 44	48/22 47/50	$280 0.31
CAMEROON	179,690 13,100,000	41 2.9	Yaoundé	English, French, African langs.	Evolving multiparty republic; Presi-dent Paul Biya	1960 45	66/43 54/58	$1,040 0.45
CANADA	3,560,220 29,100,000	77 0.7	Ottawa	English, French	Confederation with parliamentary gov't.; Prime Minister Jean Chrétien	1867 21	99 74/81	$19,600 0.93
CAPE VERDE	1,560 400,000	44 2.9	Praia	Portuguese, Crioulo	Multiparty republic; President Antonio Mascarenhas Monteiro	1975 44	61/39 67/69	$800 0.47
CENTRAL AFRICAN REPUBLIC	240,530 3,100,000	47 2.4	Bangui	French, Sangho, Arabic, others	Multiparty democracy; President Felix Ange Patasse	1960 43	33/15 42/45	$440 0.25
CHAD	486,180 6,500,000	32 2.6	N'Djamena	French, Arabic, Sara, others	In transition to democracy; President Colonel Idriss Deby	1960 41	42/18 46/49	$215 0.21

	AREA (SQ MI) POPULATION	URBAN POP. (%) POP. ANNUAL RISE (%)	CAPITAL	MAJOR LANGUAGES	FORM OF GOVERNMENT[1] AND HEAD	DATE OF INDEP.[2] % OF POP. UNDER AGE 15	LITERACY RATE (%)[3] LIFE EXPECTANCY	PER-CAPITA GDP[4] HDI
CHILE	289,110 14,000,000	85 1.7	Santiago	Spanish	Multiparty federal republic; President Eduardo Frei Ruiz-Tagle	1810 31	94/93 69/76	$2,550 0.85
CHINA	3,600,930 1,192,000,000	28 1.1	Beijing	Mandarin, other Chinese langs.	1-party Communist state; State Council Premier Li Peng	1949 28	84/62 69/72	NA 0.64
COLOMBIA	401,040 35,600,000	68 2.0	Bogotá	Spanish	Multiparty republic; President Ernesto Samper	1810 34	88/86 68/73	$1,500 0.81
COMOROS	860 500,000	28 3.5	Moroni	Arabic, French, Comoran	Parliamentary regime; President Said Mohamed Djohar	1975 48	56/40 54/59	$540 0.33
CONGO	131,850 2,400,000	41 2.6	Brazzaville	French, Lingala, Kikongo, others	Democracy under severe strain; President Pascal Lissouba	1960 44	70/44 47/51	$1,070 0.46
COSTA RICA	19,710 3,200,000	44 2.3	San José	Spanish, English	Multiparty federal republic; President José Maria Figueres	1821 36	93/93 74/79	$2,000 0.85
CÔTE D'IVOIRE	122,780 13,900,000	39 3.5	Yamoussoukro	French, Dioula, others	Multiparty republic; President Henri Konan-Bedie	1960 47	67/40 50/53	$800 0.37
CROATIA	21,830 4,800,000	51 -0.1	Zagreb	Serbo-Croatian	Parliamentary democracy; President Franjo Tudjman	1991 19	99/95 67/75	$5,600 NA
CUBA	42,400 11,100,000	73 0.8	Havana	Spanish	1-party Communist state; President Fidel Castro Ruz	1902 23	95/93 75/79	$1,370 0.67
CYPRUS	3,570 700,000	62 1.1	Nicosia	Greek, Turkish, English	Multiparty parliamentary government; President Glafcos Clerides	1960 26	96/85 74/79	NA 0.87
CZECH REPUBLIC	30,590 10,300,000	NA 0.0	Prague	Czech, Slovak	Parliamentary democracy; Prime Minister Vaclav Klaus	1993 21	NA 68/76	$7,300 NA
DENMARK	16,360 5,200,000	85 0.1	Copenhagen	Danish, Faroese, others	Multiparty parl. constitut. monarchy; Prime Minister Poul Nyrup Rasmussen	1849 17	99 73/78	$18,200 0.91
DJIBOUTI	8,950 600,000	77 3.0	Djibouti	French, Arabic, Somali, Afar	1-party parliamentary government; President Hassan Gouled Aptidon	1977 41	63/34 47/51	$1,030 0.27
DOMINICA	290 100,000	NA 1.3	Roseau	English, French patois	Multiparty parliamentary gov't.; Prime Minister Eugenia Charles	1978 31	94/94 73/79	$2,100 0.75
DOMINICAN REPUBLIC	18,680 7,800,000	60 2.2	Santo Domingo	Spanish	Multiparty centralized republic; President Joaquín Balaguer Ricardo	1844 38	85/82 65/70	$1,120 0.64
ECUADOR	106,890 10,600,000	57 2.5	Quito	Spanish, Quechua, others	Multiparty republic; President Sixto Duran-Ballen	1822 39	88/84 66/72	$1,100 0.72
EGYPT	384,340 58,900,000	45 2.3	Cairo	Arabic, English, French	Multiparty presidential regime; President Muhammad Hosni Mubarak	1922 40	63/34 60/63	$730 0.55
EL SALVADOR	8,000 5,200,000	45 2.7	San Salvador	Spanish, Nahua	Republic; President Armando Calderón Sol	1821 44	76/70 64/69	$1,060 0.54
EQUATORIAL GUINEA	10,830 400,000	37 2.6	Malabo	Spanish, pidgin Eng., Fang, others	Dictatorship; President Brig. Gen. Teodoro Obiang Nguema Mbasogo	1968 43	64/37 49/53	$380 0.27
ERITREA	48,260 3,500,000	NA 2.6	Asmera	Tigre, Kunama, others	Transitional government; President Issaias Afeworke	1993 NA	NA NA	$115 NA
ESTONIA	17,410 1,500,000	71 -0.4	Tallinn	Estonian, Latvian, others	Parliamentary republic; Prime Minister Mart Laar	1991 22	NA 65/75	NA 0.87
ETHIOPIA	376,830 55,200,000	15 3.1	Addis Ababa	Amharic, Tigrinya, others	Multiparty transitional government; President Meles Zenawi	200 49	9/0.5 50/53	$130 0.25
FIJI	7,050 800,000	39 2.0	Suva	English, Fijian, Hindustani	Parliamentary gov't. with constit. restrictions; Prime Min. Sitiveni Rabuka	1970 38	90/81 62/67	$1,900 0.79
FINLAND	117,610 5,100,000	80 0.3	Helsinki	Finnish, Swedish, others	Multiparty republic; President Martti Ahtisaari	1917 19	100 71/79	$15,900 0.91
FRANCE	212,390 58,000,000	74 0.4	Paris	French, regional dialects	Multiparty republic; President François Mitterrand	1792 20	99 73/81	$18,900 0.93
GABON	99,490 1,100,000	46 2.7	Libreville	French, Fang, Myene, others	Multiparty republic; President El Hadj Omar Bongo	1960 33	74/48 52/55	$4,200 0.52
GAMBIA	3,860 1,100,000	26 2.7	Banjul	English, Mandinka, Wolof, others	Military dictatorship; Lieutenant Yahya Jammeh	1965 45	39/16 43/47	$325 0.22

	AREA (SQ MI) POPULA-TION	URBAN POP. (%) POP. ANNUAL RISE (%)	CAPITAL	MAJOR LANGUAGES	FORM OF GOVERNMENT[1] AND HEAD	DATE OF INDEP.[2] % OF POP. UNDER AGE 15	LITERACY RATE (%)[3] LIFE EXPECT-ANCY	PER-CAPITA GDP[4] HDI
GEORGIA	26,900 5,500,000	56 0.8	Georgian, Tbilisi	Russian, Armenian, others	Constitutional democracy; Chairman of Parliament and Head of State Eduard A. Shevardnadze	1991 25	NA 69/76	NA 0.75
GERMANY	134,930 81,200,000	85 -0.1	Berlin	German	Multiparty parliamentary government; Chancellor Helmut Kohl	1990 16	99 72/79	$17,400 0.92
GHANA	88,810 16,900,000	34 3.0	Accra	English, Akan, others	Constitutional parliamentary gov't.; President Jerry John Rawlings	1957 45	70/51 54/58	$410 0.38
GREECE	50,520 10,400,000	58 0.1	Athens	Greek, English, French	Multiparty parliamentary government; Prime Minister Andreas Papandreou	1829 19	98/89 75/80	$8,200 0.87
GRENADA	130 100,000	32 2.5	St. George's	English, French patois	Multiparty parliamentary government; Prime Minister Nicholas Brathwaite	1974 43	98/98 68/72	$3,000 0.71
GUATEMALA	41,860 10,300,000	38 3.1	Guatemala	Spanish, Indian languages	Multiparty republic; military influence; President Ramiro de León Carpio	1821 45	63/47 62/67	$1,300 0.56
GUINEA	94,930 6,400,000	26 2.5	Conakry	French, various African langs. etc..	In transition to democratic system; President Brig. Gen. Lansana Conte	1958 44	35/13 41/45	$410 0.19
GUINEA-BISSAU	10,860 1,100,000	20 2.1	Bissau	Portuguese, Criolo, others	Multiparty government; President João Bernardo Vieira	1974 43	50/24 42/45	$210 0.22
GUYANA	76,000 800,000	33 1.8	Georgetown	English, Indian languages	2-party presidential regime; President Dr. Cheddi Jagan	1966 33	98/96 62/68	$370 0.58
HAITI	10,640 7,000,000	31 2.3	Port-au-Prince	French, Creole	Military-backed gov't; agreed to return power to Pres. Jean-Bertrand Aristide	1804 40	59/47 44/47	$340 0.35
HONDURAS	43,200 5,300,000	44 3.1	Tegucigalpa	Spanish, Indian languages	Republic; President Carlos Roberto Reina	1821 47	76/71 64/69	$1,090 0.52
HUNGARY	35,650 10,300,000	63 -0.3	Budapest	Hungarian, others	Multiparty parliamentary government; Prime Minister Gyula Horn	1001 19	99/98 65/74	$5,380 0.86
ICELAND	38,710 300,000	91 1.1	Reykjavík	Icelandic	Multiparty republic; Prime Minister David Oddsson	1944 25	100 75/80	$17,400 0.91
INDIA	1,147,950 911,600,000	26 1.9	New Delhi	Hindi, English, many others	Multiparty parliamentary government; Prime Minister P.V. Narasimha Rao	1947 36	62/34 57/57	$270 0.38
INDONESIA	705,190 199,700,000	31 1.6	Jakarta	Bahasa Indo-nesian, others	Republic; President General Suharto	1945 37	84/68 58/62	$680 0.58
IRAN	631,660 61,200,000	57 3.6	Tehran	Persian, Turkic, Kurdish, others	1-party Islamic republic; President Ali Akbar Hashemi-Rafsanjani	1979 47	64/43 64/65	$1,500 0.67
IRAQ	168,870 19,900,000	70 3.7	Baghdad	Arabic, Kurdish, Assyrian, others	Republic; President Saddam Hussein	1932 48	70/49 63/64	$1,940 0.61
IRELAND	26,600 3,600,000	56 0.6	Dublin	English, Gaelic	Multiparty parliamentary government; Prime Minister Albert Reynolds	1921 27	98 71/77	$12,000 0.89
ISRAEL	7,850 5,400,000	90 1.5	Jerusalem	Hebrew, Arabic, English	Multiparty parliamentary government; Prime Minister Yitzhak Rabin	1948 31	95/89 74/78	$12,100 0.90
ITALY	113,540 57,200,000	68 0.0	Rome	Italian, others	Multiparty parliamentary government; Prime Minister Silvio Berlusconi	1861 16	98/96 74/80	$17,500 0.89
JAMAICA	4,180 2,500,000	52 1.8	Kingston	English, Creole	2-party parliamentary government; Prime Minister P.J. Patterson	1962 33	98/99 71/76	$1,500 0.75
JAPAN	145,370 125,000,000	77 0.3	Tokyo	Japanese	Multiparty parl. constit. monarchy; Prime Minister Tomiichi Murayama	660 B.C. 17	99 76/82	$19,800 0.93
JORDAN	34,340 4,200,000	70 3.3	Amman	Arabic, English	Constitutional monarchy evolving to multiparty gov't.; King Hussein I	1946 41	89/70 64/70	$1,100 0.63
KAZAKHSTAN	1,049,200 17,100,000	58 1.2	Alma-Ata	Kazakh, Russian	Constitutional democracy; President Nursultan Nazarbayev	1991 31	NA 64/73	NA 0.77
KENYA	219,960 27,000,000	25 3.3	Nairobi	English, Swahili, others	In transition to democracy; Presi-dent Daniel T. arap Moi	1963 49	80/58 57/61	$320 0.43
KIRIBATI	280 76,320	NA 2.0	Tarawa	English, Gilberte e	Caretaker government, pending election results	1979 NA	NA 51/56	$525 NA
KOREA, NORTH	46,490 23,100,000	60 1.9	Pyongyang	Korean	1-party Communist state; President Kim Jong Il (status not yet official)	1948 29	99/99 66/73	$1,000 0.61

	AREA (SQ MI) POPULA-TION	URBAN POP. (%) POP. ANNUAL RISE (%)	CAPITAL	MAJOR LANGUAGES	FORM OF GOVERNMENT[1] AND HEAD	DATE OF INDEP.[2] % OF POP. UNDER AGE 15	LITERACY RATE (%)[3] LIFE EXPECT-ANCY	PER-CAPITA GDP[4] HDI
KOREA, SOUTH	38,120 44,500,000	74 1.0	Seoul	Korean, English	Multiparty republic; President Kim Young Sam	1948 24	99/94 67/75	$6,500 0.86
KUWAIT	6,880 1,300,000	NA 3.3	Kuwait	Arabic, English	Const. monarchy; Crown Prince Sa'ud al-'Abdallah al-Salim al-Sabah	1961 43	78/69 74/78	$11,100 0.81
KYRGYZSTAN	76,600 4,500,000	37 2.1	Bishkek	Kirghiz, Russian	Multiparty democracy; President Askar Akayev	1991 38	NA 65/73	NA 0.69
LAOS	89,110 4,700,000	19 2.9	Vientiane	Lao, French, English	1-party Communist state; President Nouhak Phoumsavanh	1949 45	92/76 49/52	$200 0.38
LATVIA	24,900 2,500,000	70 -0.1	Riga	Latvian, Lithu-anian, others	Parliamentary republic; President Guntis Ulmanis	1991 21	98 64/75	NA 0.86
LEBANON	3,950 3,600,000	86 2.0	Beirut	Arabic, French, others	Parliamentary republic; President Ilyas Harawi	1943 33	88/73 73/78	$1,400 0.60
LESOTHO	11,720 1,900,000	19 1.9	Maseru	Sesotho, Eng., Zulu, Xhosa	Multiparty parliamentary republic; Prime Minister Ntsu Mokhehle	1966 41	44/68 58/63	$340 0.48
LIBERIA	37,190 2,900,000	43 3.3	Monrovia	English, Niger-Congo langs.	Transitional gov't. with elections this year; President David Kpomakpor	1847 45	50/29 54/57	$400 0.32
LIBYA	679,360 5,100,000	76 3.4	Tripoli	Arabic, Italian, English	1-party military government; Colonel Mu'ammar al-Gadhafi	1951 47	75/50 62/65	$5,800 0.70
LIECHTENSTEIN	60 30,000	NA 0.8	Vaduz	German, Ale-mannic dialect	Principality; Prime Minister Mario Frick	1719 19	100/100 74/81	$22,300 NA
LITHUANIA	25,210 3,700,000	69 0.3	Vilnius	Lithuanian, Po-lish, Russian	Parliamentary republic; Prime Minister Adolfas Slezevicius	1991 22	NA 65/76	NA 0.87
LUXEMBOURG	990 400,000	86 0.3	Luxembourg	Luxembourgisch, German, others	Multiparty parl. constit. monarchy; Prime Minister Jacques Delors	1839 17	100/100 72/79	$21,700 0.91
MACEDONIA	9,930 2,100,000	54 0.8	Skopje	Macedonian, Albanian, others	Parliamentary government; President Kiro Gligorov	1991 26	94/84 70/74	$3,110 NA
MADAGASCAR	224,530 13,700,000	22 3.3	Antananarivo	French, Malagasy	Multiparty republic; President Albert Vafy	1960 45	88/73 54/57	$200 0.40
MALAWI	36,320 9,500,000	17 2.7	Lilongwe	English, Chi-chewa, others	Multipary democracy; President Muluzi Bakili	1964 48	34/12 44/44	$200 0.26
MALAYSIA	126,850 19,500,000	51 2.3	Kuala Lumpur	Malay, English, others	Multiparty parl. constit. monarchy; Prime Minister Mahathir bin Mohamad	1957 36	86/70 69/73	$2,960 0.79
MALDIVES	120 200,000	26 3.2	Male	Divehi, English	Presidential regime; President Maumoon Abdul Gayoom	1965 47	92/92 62/59	$620 0.51
MALI	471,120 9,100,000	22 3.0	Bamako	French, Bam-bara, others	Evolving multiparty government; President Alpha Oumar Konare	1960 46	41/24 44/47	$265 0.21
MALTA	120 400,000	85 0.7	Valletta	Maltese, English	2-party parliamentary government; Prime Minister Eddie Fenech Adami	1964 23	86/82 74/77	$7,600 0.84
MARSHALL ISLANDS	70 51,980	65 4.0	Majuro	English, local dia-lects, Japanese	Federal republic; President Amata Kabua	1986 51	100/88 60/63	$1,500 NA
MAURITANIA	395,840 2,300,000	39 2.9	Nouakchott	Hasaniya Arabic, Wolof, others	Republic; President Colonel Maaouya Ould Sid'Ahmed Taya	1960 44	47/21 46/50	$555 0.25
MAURITIUS	710 1,100,000	39 1.5	Port Louis	English, Creole, French, others	Multiparty republic; Prime Minister Anerood Jugnauth	1968 30	89/77 65/73	$2,300 0.78
MEXICO	736,950 91,800,000	71 2.2	Mexico City	Spanish, various Mayan languages	Multiparty federal republic; President Carlos Salinas de Gortari	1810 38	90/85 67/73	$3,600 0.80
MICRONESIA	270 100,000	26 3.0	Kolonia	English, Truk-ese, others	Federal republic; President Bailey Olter	1986 46	90/85 65/69	$1,500 NA
MOLDOVA	14,170 4,400,000	48 0.6	Chisinau (Kishinev)	Moldovan, Russian	Constitutional democracy; President Mircea Snegur	1991 28	NA 65/72	NA 0.71
MONACO	0.6 31,010	NA 0.9	Monaco	French, English, Monegasque	1-party constitutional monarchy; Prince Rainier III	1419 NA	NA 72/80	$16,000 NA
MONGOLIA	604,830 2,400,000	57 2.7	Ulaanbaatar (Ulan Bator)	Khalkha Mongol, Turkic, Russian	Multiparty democratic state; Prime Minister Puntsagiyn Jasray	1921 44	90 63/67	$800 0.61

	AREA (SQ MI) POPULATION	URBAN POP. (%) POP. ANNUAL RISE (%)	CAPITAL	MAJOR LANGUAGES	FORM OF GOVERNMENT[1] AND HEAD	DATE OF INDEP.[2] % OF POP. UNDER AGE 15	LITERACY RATE (%)[3] LIFE EXPECTANCY	PER-CAPITA GDP[4] HDI
MOROCCO	172,320 28,600,000	47 2.3	Rabat	Arabic, Berber dialects, French	Multiparty constitutional monarchy; King Hassan II	1956 40	61/38 65/69	$1,060 0.55
MOZAMBIQUE	302,740 15,800,000	27 2.7	Maputo	Portuguese, African languages	In transition to multiparty government; President Joaquím Alberto Chissano	1975 44	45/21 45/48	$115 0.25
MYANMAR	253,880 45,400,000	25 1.9	Yangon	Burmese, ethnic languages	Military regime; General Than Shwe	1948 36	89/72 57/61	$660 0.41
NAMIBIA	317,870 1,600,000	33 3.3	Windhoek	Afrikaans, German, English	Multiparty government; President Sam Nujoma	1990 45	45/31 58/60	$1,300 0.42
NAURU	8 9,880	NA 1.4	no official capital	Nauruan, English	Multiparty parliamentary government; President Bernard Dowiyogo	1968 NA	NA NA	$10,000 NA
NEPAL	52,820 22,100,000	8 2.4	Kathmandu	Nepali, many others	Multiparty parliamentary government; Prime Minister Girija Prasad Koirala	1768 44	38/13 51/51	$170 0.29
NETHERLANDS	13,100 15,400,000	89 0.4	Amsterdam	Dutch	Multiparty parl. constit. monarchy; Prime Minister Willem Kok	1579 18	99 74/80	$17,200 0.92
NEW ZEALAND	103,470 3,500,000	85 0.9	Wellington	English, Maori	Multiparty parliamentary government; Prime Minister James Bolger	1907 23	99 72/78	$14,900 0.91
NICARAGUA	45,850 4,300,000	62 2.9	Managua	Spanish, English, Indian languages	Republic; President Violeta Chamorro	1821 46	57/57 60/66	$425 0.58
NIGER	489,070 8,800,000	15 3.4	Niamey	French, Hausa, Djerma	Democratic government; President Mahamane Ousmane	1960 49	40/17 45/48	$290 0.21
NIGERIA	351,650 98,100,000	16 3.1	Abuja	English, Hausa, Yoruba, others	Military government; General Sani Abacha	1960 45	62/40 53/55	$300 0.35
NORWAY	118,470 4,300,000	72 0.4	Oslo	Norwegian, Lapp, Finnish	Multiparty parl. constit. monarchy; Prime Minister Gro Harlem Brundtland	1905 19	99 74/80	$17,700 0.93
OMAN	82,030 1,900,000	12 4.9	Muscat	Arabic, English, Balochi, others	Absolute monarchy; Sultan and Prime Minister Qaboos bin Sa'id Al Sa'id	1650 36	58/24 70/73	$6,670 0.65
PAKISTAN	297,640 126,400,000	28 2.8	Islamabad	Urdu, English, Punjabi, others	Multiparty parliamentary government; Prime Minister Benazir Bhutto	1947 44	47/21 59/61	$410 0.39
PANAMA	29,340 2,500,000	49 1.8	Panama City	Spanish, English	Multiparty republic; President Ernesto Perez Balladares	1903 35	88/88 71/75	$2,400 0.82
PAPUA NEW GUINEA	174,850 4,000,000	13 2.3	Port Moresby	Pidgin English, Motu, others	Multiparty parliamentary government; Prime Minister Paias Wingti	1975 40	65/38 54/56	$850 0.41
PARAGUAY	153,400 4,800,000	51 2.7	Asunción	Spanish, Guarani	Multiparty federal republic; President Juan Carlos Wasmosy	1811 40	92/88 65/69	$1,500 0.68
PERU	494,210 22,900,000	71 2.0	Lima	Spanish, Quechua, Aymara	Republic under state of emergency; President Alberto Kenyo Fujimori	1821 38	92/29 63/67	$1,100 0.64
PHILIPPINES	115,120 68,700,000	44 2.4	Manila	Filipino, English	Multiparty federal republic; President Fidel Ramos	1946 39	90/90 63/66	$860 0.62
POLAND	117,550 38,600,000	62 0.3	Warsaw	Polish	Multiparty parliamentary government; President Lech Walesa	1918 25	99/98 66/75	$4,400 0.82
PORTUGAL	35,500 9,900,000	34 0.2	Lisbon	Portuguese	Multiparty parliamentary government; Prime Minister Anibal Cavaco Silva	1910 20	89/82 71/78	$9,000 0.84
QATAR	4,250 500,000	91 1.0	Doha	Arabic, English	Absolute monarchy; Prime Minister Khalifa bin Hamad Al Thani	1971 23	77/72 70/74	$17,000 0.80
ROMANIA	88,930 22,700,000	54 -0.1	Bucharest	Romanian, Hungarian, German	Parliamentary democracy; President Ion Iliescu	1947 22	96 67/73	$2,700 0.73
RUSSIA	6,592,800 147,800,000	73 -0.2	Moscow	Russian, other languages	Constitutional democracy; President Boris Yeltsin	1991 22	NA 62/74	NA 0.86
RWANDA	9,530 7,700,000	5 2.3	Kigali	Kinyarwanda, French, Kiswahili	Temporary military government; no leader	1962 48	64/37 45/48	$290 0.27
SAINT KITTS AND NEVIS	140 40,000	49 1.3	Basseterre	English	Multiparty parliamentary government; Prime Minister Kennedy A. Simmonds	1983 32	98/98 66/71	$3,500 0.73
SAINT LUCIA	240 100,000	46 2.0	Castries	English, French patois	Multiparty parliamentary government; Prime Minister John Compton	1979 44	65/69 68/75	$1,650 0.71

	AREA (SQ MI) POPULATION	URBAN POP. (%) POP. ANNUAL RISE (%)	CAPITAL	MAJOR LANGUAGES	FORM OF GOVERNMENT[1] AND HEAD	DATE OF INDEP.[2] % OF POP. UNDER AGE 15	LITERACY RATE (%)[3] LIFE EXPECTANCY	PER-CAPITA GDP[4] HDI
SAINT VINCENT AND THE GRENADINES	150 100,000	25 1.7	Kingstown	English, French patois	Multiparty parliamentary government; Prime Minister James F. Mitchell	1979 37	96/96 69/72	$1,500 0.73
SAN MARINO	20 20,000	90 0.3	San Marino	Italian	Multiparty republic; Secretary of State Gabriele Gatti	301 16	96/95 73/79	$20,000 NA
SÃO TOMÉ AND PRINCIPE	370 100,000	41 2.5	São Tomé	Portuguese	Multiparty republic; President Miguel Trovoada	1975 41	73/42 61/65	$315 0.41
SAUDI ARABIA	830,000 18,000,000	79 3.2	Riyadh	Arabic	Absolute monarchy; King and Prime Min. Fahd bin 'Abd al-'Aziz Al Sa'ud	1932 43	73/48 69/72	$6,500 0.74
SENEGAL	74,340 8,200,000	39 2.7	Dakar	French, Wolof, other langs.	Multiparty parliamentary government; President Abdou Diouf	1960 47	52/25 48/50	$780 0.32
SERBIA AND MONTENEGRO	26,940 10,500,000	47 0.4	Belgrade	Serbo-Croatian, Albanian	Parliamentary democracy; President Zoran Lilic	1992 23	95/83 69/75	$3,000 NA
SEYCHELLES	100 100,000	50 1.5	Victoria	English, French, Creole	Multiparty republic; President France Albert René	1976 35	85 65/73	$5,200 0.68
SIERRA LEONE	27,650 4,600,000	32 2.7	Freetown	English, Krio, Mende, Temne	Military government; Chairman Captain Valentine E. M. Strasser	1961 45	31/11 41/45	$330 0.21
SINGAPORE	240 2,900,000	100 1.2	Singapore	Chinese, Malay, Tamil, English	Parliamentary government; Prime Minister Goh Chok Tong	1965 23	93/84 72/77	$16,500 0.84
SLOVAKIA	18,790 5,300,000	57 0.4	Bratislava	Slovak, Hungarian	Parliamentary democracy; Prime Minister Jozef Moravcik	1993 25	100 67/75	$6,100 NA
SLOVENIA	7,820 2,000,000	49 0.1	Ljubljana	Slovenian, Serbo-Croatian, other	Multiparty democracy; Prime Minister Janez Drnovsek	1991 20	99/99 69/77	$10,700 NA
SOLOMON ISLANDS	10,810 400,000	13 3.7	Honiara	Melanesian pidgin, many others	Multiparty parliamentary government; Prime Minister Francis Billy Hilly	1978 47	62/45 NA	$600 0.43
SOMALIA	242,220 9,800,000	24 3.2	Mogadishu	Somali, Arabic, Italian, English	No functioning government or leader	1960 47	36/14 45/49	NA 0.22
SOUTH AFRICA	471,440 41,200,000	57 2.6	Cape Town, Pretoria, & Bloemfontein	Eng., Afrikaans, Zulu, Xhosa, Sotho, Tswana	Multiparty parliamentary government; President Nelson Mandela	1910 39	78/75 62/67	$2,800 0.65
SPAIN	192,830 39,200,000	78 0.1	Madrid	Spanish, Catalan, others	Constitutional monarchy; Prime Minister Felipe González Marquez	1492 19	97/93 73/80	$13,200 0.89
SRI LANKA	24,950 17,900,000	22 1.5	Colombo	Sinhala, Tamil, English	Multiparty republic; President Dingiri Banda Wijetunga	1948 35	91/81 70/75	$440 0.66
SUDAN	917,370 28,200,000	23 3.1	Khartoum	Arabic, many regional langs.	Military government; Lieutenant General Umar Hasan Ahmad al-Bashir	1956 46	43/12 52/54	$184 0.28
SURINAME	60,230 400,000	70 1.6	Paramaribo	Dutch, English, Sranan Tongo	Federal republic; President Ronald R. Venetiaan	1975 41	95/95 66/71	$3,300 0.68
SWAZILAND	6,640 800,000	23 3.2	Mbabane & Lobamba	English, siSwati	Monarchy; King Mswati III	1968 47	57/54 52/60	$800 0.51
SWEDEN	158,930 8,800,000	83 0.3	Stockholm	Swedish, Lapp, Finnish	Multiparty parl. constitutional monarchy; Prime Minister Carl Bildt	1809 18	99 75/80	$16,900 0.93
SWITZERLAND	15,360 7,000,000	68 0.3	Bern	German, French, Italian, others	Multiparty federal state; President Otto Stich	1291 16	99 74/81	$22,300 0.93
SYRIA	71,070 14,000,000	51 3.7	Damascus	Arabic, Kurdish, others	Republic under military regime; President Hafez al-Assad	1946 48	78/51 65/67	$2,300 0.73
TAIWAN	13,900 21,100,000	75 1.0	Taipei	Mandarin Chinese, others	Multiparty presidential regime; President Li Teng-hui	1947 26	91 72/77	$10,000 NA
TAJIKISTAN	55,300 5,900,000	31 2.9	Dushanbe	Tajik	Coalition formed during ongoing civil war; President Emomili Rakhmanov	1991 43	NA 67/72	NA 0.63
TANZANIA	342,100 29,800,000	21 3.4	Dar es Salaam	Swahili, English	In transition to multiparty republic; President Ali Hassan Mwinyi	1964 47	62/31 49/52	$260 0.31
THAILAND	197,250 59,400,000	19 1.4	Bangkok	Thai, English, ethnic languages	Constitutional monarchy; Prime Minister Chuan Leekpai	1238 29	96/90 67/72	$1,800 0.80
TOGO	21,000 4,300,000	29 3.6	Lomé	French, Ewe, Mina, others	Multiparty state in transition; President Gen. Gnassingbe Eyadema	1960 49	56/31 54/58	$400 0.31

	AREA (SQ MI) POPULATION	URBAN POP. (%) POP. ANNUAL RISE (%)	CAPITAL	MAJOR LANGUAGES	FORM OF GOVERNMENT[1] AND HEAD	DATE OF INDEP.[2] % OF POP. UNDER AGE 15	LITERACY RATE (%)[3] LIFE EXPECTANCY	PER-CAPITA GDP[4] HDI
TONGA	288 103,950	NA 0.8	Nuku'alofa	Tongan, English	Constitutional monarchy; King Taufa'ahau Tupou IV	1970 NA	100/100 69/74	$900 NA
TRINIDAD AND TOBAGO	1,980 1,300,000	69 1.2	Port-of-Spain	English, Hindi, French, Spanish	2-party parliamentary government; Prime Minister Patrick A.M. Manning	1962 32	97/93 69/74	$3,800 0.86
TUNISIA	59,980 8,700,000	59 1.9	Tunis	Arabic, French	Multiparty republic; President Zine El Abidine Ben Ali	1956 37	74/56 67/69	$1,650 0.69
TURKEY	297,150 61,800,000	61 2.2	Ankara	Turkish, Kurdish, Arabic	Multiparty parliamentary government; Prime Minister Tansu Ciller	1923 35	90/71 64/70	$3,670 0.74
TURKMENISTAN	188,500 4,100,000	45 2.6	Ashkhabad	Turkmen, Russian, others	1-party state dominated by president; President Saparmurad Niyazov	1991 40	NA 63/70	NA 0.70
TUVALU	10 9,670	NA 1.7	Funafuti	Tuvaluan, English	Parliamentary government; Prime Minister Kamuta Latasi	1978 NA	95 60/63	$530 NA
UGANDA	77,050 19,800,000	11 3.0	Kampala	English, Luganda, others	In transition to democracy; President Yoweri Kaguta Museveni	1962 47	62/35 41/43	$300 0.27
UKRAINE	233,100 51,500,000	68 -0.2	Kiev	Ukrainian, Russian, others	Parliamentary democracy; President Leonid Kuchma	1991 21	NA 64/74	NA 0.82
UNITED ARAB EMIRATES	32,280 1,700,000	83 1.9	Abu Dhabi	Arabic, Persian, English, others	Federation of member emirates; Pres. Zayid bin Sultan Al Nuhayyan	1971 32	70/63 70/74	$13,800 0.77
UNITED KINGDOM (GREAT BRITAIN)	93,280 58,400,000	92 0.2	London	English, Welsh, Scottish Gaelic	Multiparty parliamentary constitutional monarchy; Prime Minister John Major	1801 19	99 73/79	$15,900 0.92
UNITED STATES	3,539,230 260,800,000	75 0.7	Washington, D.C.	English, Spanish, others	Multiparty federal republic; President Bill (William Jefferson) Clinton	1776 22	98/98 72/79	$23,400 0.92
URUGUAY	67,490 3,200,000	89 0.8	Montevideo	Spanish	Multiparty republic; President Luis Alberto Lacalle	1828 26	97/96 70/76	$3,100 0.86
UZBEKISTAN	172,700 22,100,000	40 2.7	Tashkent	Uzbek, Russian, others	Authoritarian regime moving toward democracy; President Islam Karimov	1991 41	NA 66/72	NA 0.66
VANUATU	4,710 200,000	18 2.9	Port-Vila	English, French, Bislama	Multiparty parliamentary government; Prime Minister Maxime Carlot Korman	1980 44	57/48 NA	$900 0.49
VATICAN CITY	109 acres 811	NA 1.2	Vatican City	Italian, Latin, others	No political parties; papal state; Pope John Paul II	1929 —	100 NA	NA NA
VENEZUELA	340,560 21,300,000	84 2.6	Caracas	Spanish, Indian languages	Multiparty federal republic; President Rafael Caldera	1811 38	87/90 67/73	$2,800 0.82
VIETNAM	125,670 73,100,000	21 2.3	Hanoi	Vietnamese, French, others	1-party Communist state; Prime Minister Vo Van Kiet	1945 39	92/84 63/67	$230 0.51
WESTERN SAMOA	1,090 200,000	21 2.6	Apia	Samoan, English	Parliamentary republic; Prime Minister Tofilau Eti Alesana	1962 41	97/97 64/69	$690 NA
YEMEN	203,850 12,900,000	31 3.4	Sanaa	Arabic	Republic; President Lieutenant General 'Ali 'Abdallah Salih	1990 51	53/26 53/55	$775 0.32
ZAIRE	875,520 42,500,000	40 3.3	Kinshasa	French, Lingala, Swahili, others	Evolving toward multiparty system; President Mobutu Sese Seko	1960 45	84/61 50/53	$235 0.34
ZAMBIA	287,020 9,100,000	49 2.8	Lusaka	English, many African langs.	Multiparty system; President Frederick Chiluba	1964 48	81/65 44/45	$550 0.351
ZIMBABWE	149,290 11,200,000	27 3.0	Harare	English, Shona, Sindebele	1-party parliamentary gov't.; Executive President Robert Gabriel Mugabe	1980 48	74/60 54/57	$545 0.47

NA: Figure(s) not available.

FOOTNOTES
[1]**Form of government and head:** Some countries listed here as having one- or two-party systems may have other political parties that play little or no role in governing. Some listed as being multiparty—the U.S., for example—may have a number of political parties, but only one or two that play a significant role in governing. [2]**Date of independence:** The most recent date when each nation won control of its internal and external affairs, or when smaller areas joined to form a larger nation. [3]**Literacy rate:** If two figures are shown, the first is for males, the second for females. A single figure is for the population as a whole. Experts doubt some estimates. [4]**Per-capita gross domestic product:** Given in U.S. dollars. [5]Transfer of power to occur by October 15, 1994, by an agreement reached September 18 between U.S. negotiators and Haiti's military rulers. [6]Ernesto Zedillo Ponce de León will be sworn in as Mexico's new president on December 1.

SOURCES
For area, population, urban population, population annual rise, percent of population under 15 years, and life expectancy: *1994 World Population Data Sheet* (Washington, D.C.: Population Reference Bureau, Inc.) • For capital, major languages, date of independence, literacy rate, and per-capita GDP: *The World Factbook 1993* (Washington, D.C.: Central Intelligence Agency) • For form of government and head: *The World Factbook 1993* and the U.S. Department of State • For HDI: *Human Development Report 1994* (The United Nations Development Programme).

All data are up-to-date as of September 8, 1994   *Reprinted by permission, Junior Scholastic Magazine.*

INDEX

Julius Caesar. See Caesar, Julius
Juno (Roman god), 23
Jupiter (Roman god), 23
Justinian, Byzantine emperor, 38, 39
Justinian Code, 38, 39

k

Kamakura Shogunate, 36
Kammu, Emperor of Japan, 36
Kangaba, 45
Kennedy, John F., 107
Kennedy, Robert F., 107
Kenyatta, Jomo, 107
Khayyam, Omar. See Omar
    Khayyam
Khoikhoi (people), 53
Khoisan (people), 53
Khorsabad, 5
Khrushchev, Nikita, 106
Kiev, 86
Kievan Period, 86
King, Martin Luther, Jr., 107
kings. See absolute monarchy;
    names of specific kings
knights, 73
Koran, 41
Korea, 36, 96
Korean War, 100, 105
Koumbi, 44
Kremlin, 86
Kublai Khan, 34
Kukulcan (Mayan god), 56
Kukya, 46
Kush, 43
Kuwait, 109

l

labor unions. *See* Trade unions
Lafayette, Marquis de, 84
languages
    ancient Indian, 30
    ancient Roman, 24
    Inca, 60
    Persian, 30
    South Africa, 53
Lao-tzu, 27, 35
Latin America. See Central America;

South America; specific countries
Latin language, 24
laws
    ancient Roman, 24
    Babylonian, 4
    British labor, 89
    Justinian Code, 38, 39
    Napoleonic Code, 85
League of Nations, 93, 94, 95
Lebanon, 7
Lenin, Vladimir, 90
Leo III, Pope, 72, 73
Leo X, Pope, 79
Leonardo da Vinci, 77
libraries
    first, 5
    Muslim, 41
Lighthouse, Pharos, 25
literature
    ancient Greece, 18
    ancient India, 28, 29
    ancient Rome, 24
    Japanese, 36, 37
    Muslim, 41
    Renaissance, 78
Lloyd George, David, 94
Locke, John, 84
Long River, 32
loom
    ancient Egyptian, 14
    waterpowered, 89
    See also textiles
Louis VII, King of France, 74
Louis XIII, King of France, 83
Louis XIV, King of France, 83
Louis XVI, King of France, 84
Lusitania (ship), 91
Luther, Martin, 72, 79
Lutherans, 79
Luxembourg, 96

m

MacArthur, Douglas, 100, 105
Machiavelli, Niccolò, 78
Madero, Francisco, 67
Magellan, Ferdinand, 82
Magna Carta, 75
Mahabharata, 29

Mahmud II, Ottoman sultan, 42
Mali, 45
Manchu dynasty, 34
Manchuria, 95, 96
Mandate of Heaven, 32
Mandela, Nelson, 43, 54, 109
Mandingo (people), 45
manor, 73
mansa, 45
Mansa Musa, King of Mali, 43, 45
Mao Tse-tung, 105, 108
Marcos, Ferdinand, 107, 109
Marcus Aurelius, 21
Maria Theresa, Archduchess of
    Austria, 83
Mark Antony, 14
Marne, Battle of, 91
Mars (Roman god), 23
Marx, Karl, 35, 90
Maryland, 63
Massachusetts, 63
mathematics
    ancient Egypt, 10
    ancient Greece, 18
    ancient India, 29
    Incan counting system, 60
    Mayan, 56, 57
    Muslim, 41
    Renaissance, 78
    Roman, 24
    Sumerian, 3
Mauryan Empire, 28
Mausoleum, 25
Maximilian, Emperor of Mexico, 66
Mayan civilization, 55, 56–57
    accomplishments, 57
    gods, 56
Mecca, 41
Medes, 5
Medici family, 77
medicine
    ancient Greece, 18
    ancient India, 29
    Muslim, 41
    Renaissance, 78
Mehmet II, Ottoman sultan, 42
Meiji Restoration, 37
Memphis (Egypt), 12
Menes, King of Egypt, 12